The Jedi Academy Online Presents:
The Jedi Religion

A 21ˢᵀ Century Search for Spiritual Answers

THE JEDI ACADEMY ONLINE PRESENTS:
THE JEDI RELIGION

A 21ST CENTURY SEARCH FOR SPIRITUAL ANSWERS

Kevin Trout
The Jedi Academy Online

jediacademyonline.com
Valencia, California

Publisher: CreateSpace.com
The Jedi Academy Online
Valencia CA. 91354
USA
Telephone Number: (On Request)
Web Site: http://jediacademyonline.com
E-Mail: admin@jediacademyonline.com
Copyright © 2013 The Jedi Academy Online

All Rights Reserved. No part of this publication may be reproduced, stored in a retrieval system or transmitted in any form by any means without prior permission of the copyright owner.
Inquires Should be Made to the Jedi Academy Online.

Every effort has been made to ensure that this book is free from error or omissions. However, the Publisher, the Author, the Editor or their respective employees or agents, shall not accept responsibility for injury, loss or damage occasioned to any person acting or refraining from action as a result of material in this book whether or not such injury, loss or damage is in any way due to any negligent act or omission, breach of duty or default on the part of the Publisher, the Author, the Editor or their respective employees or agents.

Acknowledgments, References, and Disclaimers:
George Lucas, Lucasfilms LTD., and Disney Inc. - All Star Wars related material Copyright and Trademark of Lucasfilms LTD. and Disney Inc. All Rights Reserved.
Power of the Jedi Sourcebook – Copyright 2002 Lucasfilms LTD. All Rights Reserved.
Star Wars Roleplaying Guide 2nd Edition – Copyright 1996 Lucasfilms LTD. All Rights Reserved.
Jedi Apprentice Series - Jude Watson. Copyright Lucasfilms LTD. All Rights Reserved.
Jedi Academy Online – Copyright 2007-2013 Outlaw Kings Productions
I'd like to give Special Thanks to: Carolyn and Dennis Blundell, Jaden Palmer, the entire JAO membership, and to Shelley Jane Reece.

Author: Kevin Trout
Title: The Jedi Academy Online Presents: The Jedi Religion.
ISBN-13: 978-0615873480
ISBN-10: 0615873480

Editor: Kevin Trout
Cover Design: Kevin Trout © 2013
Page Design: Kevin Trout © 2013
Printed and Bound: CreateSpace and Amazon.com

This Book is Dedicated to my families:
My parents, my Jedi family, and my sanity-savior Patrick. Without each of you none of this would be possible.

Preface

I think we must quote whenever we feel that the allusion is interesting or helpful or amusing. ~ Cliff Fadiman

  I offer this as a warning more than a Preface. American-English is my native language and I am horrible at it. My writing skills were improved by my online interactions, but that type of improvement has a limit. It is like saying I learned to drive by driving in a demolition derby. I certainly developed my own voice, if you will, through my continual writings online. However that voice has a limited vocabulary and horrible grammar. If the Jedi is a subject that interests you then you will find information of value within this book. You will, of course, have to put up with my sub-par typing skills and continual grammatical errors. If the subject of Jedi does not interest you and you are reading this as a favor to a friend or family member then you have my sincerest apologies and deepest sympathies. Forewarned is forearmed and you have been warned.
  The book itself is a personal commentary on the Jedi Lifestyle. Some may use the term Jediism or the Jedi Religion, though I personally do not subscribe to such labels and find them unnecessary. The title of this book is listed as such for purely marketing purposes. Though make no mistake, I do touch on Jedi as a religion and make a case for those who do subscribe to such labels. Fact is a Jedi practices self-honesty and values honesty. In the spirit of that I am noting my personal disfavor of the religious label. While I do not claim the Jedi as my religion I could technically fall under the Jediism label. One could easily make the argument that I follow the Jedi Religion, but I simply do not apply the label to myself. I prefer Jedi rather than Jediism or Jedi Realism. If you consider yourself a Jedi you need not worry about 'isms' here. Realism, Jediism, I do not bother with either of these labels throughout the book. Jedi are Jedi, we all have the same

core values. We have the same base practices and we have the same grand goals. So I'll be doing away with the glass walls of segregation for this book. You can pick up the Jedi Circle book if you feel the desire to delve into the semantic issue of Jedi Religion more.

What you will find in *this* book is simple personal insights from myself and my experiences. I share some of my journey later on in the book. What brought me to the Jedi and why I stuck with it. A quick summary is that I have been a part of the online Jedi Community for over 15 years and been studying the ideals of the fictional Jedi for over 20 years. I simply wanted to share more openly about this wonderful path I have lived. So this book is my way of reflecting and giving thanks for the journey I have been on. I have fought, cried, bled, laughed, celebrated, and felt defeated with the Jedi and our collective community. I have grown as an individual, I have lost my path, found it again, and through the good and bad times I have always felt at home with the Jedi.

That is what you will find within this book. One Jedi's viewpoint on a path that has helped shape a life. I will share those core practices, ideals, and goals I mentioned. So you will find something a bit more tangible than my simple ramblings on the Jedi. In the end however, this is simply one voice out of many, offering some insights to whoever is curious enough to pick them up. If this book piques your interest I highly recommend seeking out a Jedi group online or off. You can find information on such groups in the last section of this book.

Table of Contents

Introduction	1
The Search	7
Sorting Fact from Fiction	10
Jedi as a Religion	19
Jedi Ideals	29
Jedi Goals	43
Jedi Practices	53
My Journey	66
Closing Thoughts	78
Resources	81

Introduction

I love those who yearn for the impossible. ~ Johann Wolfgang von Goethe

There is probably nothing better which highlights humanity's diversity than our belief systems. Pick a belief system and you'll still find sects, branches, and off-shoots within that singular label. From Christianity to Wiccan, there is a clear reflection of our differences. As humanity has grown so has our understanding of our various beliefs. More and more there is an agreement that while our labels are different, it is simply looking at the same thing through a different lens. One of the major tools which has lead to this understanding is the internet. The free exchange of knowledge, opinion, and experiences, has allow millions of people access to information previously unavailable. While you won't find many comparisons to the Renaissance era of Italy, certainly the free access to information has shown value to human growth. People are evolving spiritually and humanity as a whole is benefiting from a more accepting approach.

Of course it is not all sunshine and rainbows on or because of the internet. Humans are ingenious creatures and whatever can be used for positive, people will find a way to use it for the negative. Bigotry has hardly been eradicated, prejudice is not a thing of the past, and certainly allowing people to hide in anonymity seems to brings forth more hostility than is necessary (comments section on youtube is proof of that). Yet evolution is not a rapid process. Growth and change takes time, it takes effort, and is not always noticeable right away. Still a dialogue has begun, we are seeing the ability to talk calmly about our differences is a viable option. Not only viable, but beneficial and providing positive results. We can see that while we differ in labels we share common ground, common ideals. All beliefs have an idea of living a quality and happy life. Ethics, self-betterment, living a healthy, productive, and vibrant life, these are things which the majority of us can agree with. An idea that there is something bigger than ourselves worth pursuing in our lives. Now whether that is a deity or simply the scientific nature of the universe (not that I feel those are mutually exclusive) we can appreciate the beauty and wonder of the world. We want to experience it, to enjoy laughter, to succeed in life, to live a "good life." Those ideals are not bound to any specific belief or religion. This is extremely evident when we begun to open our eyes and minds to other belief systems in our world (the old and the new).

While the internet has given us this chance to explore bigger ideas and play philosopher online, it has also given us plenty of distractions as well. The access to various media entertainment is simply everywhere. Entertainment has been an important part of humanity from the beginning. At least that is my take. Whether or not the flood of entertainment available to us is beneficial or not is a debate for another time. However certainly throughout human history, entertainment has played a pivotal role. I highly doubt there is any point in time in which humans did not have some form of down-time. From singing, dancing, writing, story-telling, sports, painting, there is always something.

It is this mixture of information and entertainment that really builds a well-balanced view. The internet provides that balance, though most of us probably lean towards entertainment more than study and research. Even with that imbalance there is a noticeable shift in thinking and viewpoints in the world. The younger generation may not inspire some people, but there is a general theme of greater acceptance and understanding. There is a new outlook that we aren't as different as some would have us believe. Not a new concept, but certainly one that has taken time to gain traction. Many have sought to get the message out, through plays, through novels, through song, and paintings. Same message, new medium, and more importantly a much wider audience. That is the key difference here. In its time, how many people heard the message from The Merchant of Venice? *"If you prick us do we not bleed? If you tickle us do we not laugh? If you poison us do we not die?"* Yet now the audience is much wider, much more accessible, put that on an internet meme, slap George Takei's name on it and how many do you think will see it? This medium has created something unique to our era. Something our entertainment has been doing for millennia, but with a slightly different effect these days.

One thing our various entertainment has provided throughout our history is inspiration. Story-tellers have been awing us with grand adventures since the beginning and just as long there have been those who listen and decided to make the story a reality. They listened in wonder and thought, why not? Why can't I do the same? This sense of mystery and aspiration is what lead to our discoveries in the world. We dreamed about flying before we ever could. We dreamed about exploring the depth of the ocean. We dreamed about going to space. Continually our dreams seemed like these fictional ideals which could never be done. Yet as we know now, one by one we made our dreams a reality. This is simply the more known and general accomplishments. Yet on a personal level people have been pursuing their dreams and making them a reality since we as a species could dream. Our imaginations have provided us with lofty goals which we have managed to accomplish given time. Not everyone is successful in such endeavors, but enough are that we acknowledge the importance of not simply writing off our grand desires. We accept that dreams can come true and that given enough hard work, resources, and time, truly anything is possible.

That is the power of asking why not. That is the power the story-tellers have always held. Jules Verne, H.G. Wells, they inspired and some of their general concepts became reality. We see the Newspad in *2001: A Space Odyssey* become a reality with the iPad and a Newsweek app. There is nothing out of our grasp as a whole. We continually break barriers and in doing so we unleash new ideas, new stories, and new dreams. It is a cycle of inspiration which is not limited to the physical sciences. Sure our scientific advancements are the best tangible example of fiction

turned reality. Yet what we are discovering is that such inspiration is not limited to such fields. Simply living a more productive and beneficial life is something that is being sought through the online medium. Stories of human nature, of human success in a variety of forms has inspired people to live more positive lives.
Sometimes these stories are based off of reality, people who have overcome adversity and triumphed. Sometimes these are fictional stories which don't even take place on planet Earth. Yet the concepts, the message is the same, you get to chose who you want to be. You get to steer your life in the direction you desire. You will face obstacles, you will deal with unexpected challenges, but ultimately it boils down to you and your choices.

    A rather long build up to simply point out there is validity in the many wild labels people have chosen to their lives under. There will always be those that lose touch with reality, but that does not diminish the value of exploring ways to improve the self. When something challenges you to look at your physical, emotional, mental, spiritual, social, environmental, and even financial well-being, can it truly be dismissed simply because of the name/label used? I laugh at myself daily for the name I have placed upon myself, labels can be silly that way. I do not laugh at the concepts however. My path has been a useful and beneficial source in my life. While I have not always made the proper choices, I can say that I am a much better person and have a much better life because of the Path I follow.

    People are no longer just accepting the old ideas. People are questioning, they are poking and prodding the old beliefs seeking to see if they truly have merit. For some they simply do not, for others they are a bit incomplete, and for others still, they are perfect. So certain people went searching for something that spoke to them and they attached themselves to a label that may be unfamiliar to the general public. That label may be Jedi, it may be Matrixism, it might be Otherkin, many fictionally inspired paths out there. Dreams of something beyond our grasp, which inspire one to reach for something more, to improve their lives. It is different and it is relatively new. Though it does offer a way for people to explore important and core concepts in humanity (in general) and within themselves as individuals.

Taking our inspiration and using it as a means of self-betterment is a delicate balance. As noted, some people lose that balance and it can stop being beneficial. What I want to impress upon you is the simple fact that a label alone should not be a basis for judgment. The questions must be deeper, do not worry about public perception just yet. Instead question to ensure that actual growth, development, and beneficial progress is being pursued. Can the path, can the label, provide a strong foundation for a individual to grow in a productive manner? Is it healthy physically, mentally, emotionally, etc.? Does it offer a safe, stimulating, and nurturing environment for a person to advance within their life? Not all places can answer yes to such and I mean that regardless of label; even certain churches cannot answer in the affirmative to such questions.

Personally I see the beauty that our culture has brought. Sure there are negatives, as I said people will find a way to twist things. Our society, our world, is changing, it is moving to a more connected atmosphere. All of that diversity can be scary and some people are feeling a bit out of sorts. Yet it is forcing people to acknowledge that different does not equal bad. Our diversity is a strength, our ability to connect with people all over the world in real-time is a strength. We are growing into a stronger version of humanity because of this and all we need to do is keep a proper balance. Small groups born of the internet era, like the Jedi, will have an effect and play a part in this ever-evolving culture. The Jedi won't be wearing robes and wielding lightsabers into battle, but we will be a voice. We will be reminding people that while you may not understand the label, the ideals behind it still have value. That just because you do not understand something, does not mean it is worthless. That regardless of the label you wear, self-betterment is a worthwhile goal and does have an effect on bettering the world around you. We will remind people that you cannot dismiss the voices of reason and compassion simply because you do not understand, agree with, or like the label they wear. This is my inspiration, this is the dream I chase. That we, as a race, embrace our differences and become stronger for them. A dream born from a science-fiction tale I enjoyed as a child. Does that really make it any less valid or any less worth pursuing?

The Search

Learning is the beginning of wealth. Learning is the beginning of health. Learning is the beginning of spirituality. Searching and learning is where the miracle process all begins. ~ Jim Rohn

It is interesting to be in a transitional generation. I am a part of Generation X which really got to see the contrast of technological advancement. Growing up we were able to see the steady advancement of various comforts. Beta tapes to VHS to Laser-Disc to DVD to Blu-Ray. Cassettes to CD to MP3. Commodore 64 to the NES and now the X-box One. And who can forget, compare the rotary dial phones to iPhones. Progress has condensed information and made it much more accessible. It is said we live in the information-age and with a device that fits in your pocket and has access to nearly-unlimited knowledge it seems an apt description. So is it truly any wonder that our search for spiritual answers has evolved as well?

I honestly cannot imagine how one began looking for answers 100 years ago, outside of the answers they were given as a child. It seems those stories of people traveling the world would be the most accurate. That you had to venture out into the world and find unique places that would offer spiritual exploration. Now regardless of age, money, location, you can jump on the computer and start your search for something more. Information is a mouse click or even a voice command away. You can easily read and search through the Holy Bible online. You can scroll through the Qur'an, the Torah, the Tao te Ching. You can read the various Sutras online. Learn the difference between Zen Buddhism and Shingon Buddhism. How about the Noosphere? Knowledge and information is right there to be gained for your spiritual quest. This allows us to really understand where other people are coming from. To understand their beliefs, whether or not we agree is an entirely different book.

The point here is that spiritually is rising to the forefront because of ease of access. We are able to see more clearly the threads that tie these different beliefs together. We notice the common ideals of compassion, of living an ethical and moral life, of being of service to our race as a whole. The flip side is religions, the major organizations, are facing a change in generational thinking. Some of the core teachings which deal with how life was back when the original documents were created doesn't not resonate in today's world. Equality is a much more accepted concept among humanity these days. It is a highly valued ideal that no one should be ostracized if they are living a decent life. If they live by concepts of love, service, respect, accountability, of spreading happiness, then why would any power in the universe deny them blessings?

People come online daily to reaffirm there place in life. They are looking for something more. A resource that church (temple, synagogue, etc.) used to fill is being replaced by the virtual search. This isn't to say that traditional institutions are lacking or failing, but simply that one has greater access to a variety of beliefs on the internet. Due to this focus and rise of online spirituality people have wanted to tie in other ideals which have inspired them. With the great mix of cultures online you can find yourself mixing and matching ideals and concepts. As an example, a Taoist practice may encourage and fit perfectly with one's current Wiccan practices. An Atheist may find some Buddhist practices as a great supplement to their lifestyle. Mixing concepts found throughout the world in an effort to lead a more productive life.

A Christian may thoroughly be inspired by their religion and yet also find that popular pop-culture speaks on the same level. So they seek to find a balance, to merge the two concepts. To use one to explore the other. I knew a person within the online Jedi community who felt the Jedi Path offered the best way to explore Christian concepts and beliefs. It was his way of exploring his religion that was dear to him, but in a different manner than one may find at Bible study. It worked for him and helped him really embrace his faith. This is part of what helped build the Jedi Community in general. A mixture of people with varying beliefs (religiously, philosophically, etc.) coming together under a common terminology to explore the grand questions that often surround life. By having that cushion of accepted terms which blanket many concepts at once, e.g. the Force being something which one can equate with just about any religious (and non-religious) belief, a lot petty arguments can be avoided. It becomes less about semantic issues on which word is right and more about the common underlying themes throughout all spiritual practices.

Of course the internet is still the internet and anonymity still breeds hostile speech. I do not wish to make it seem as if we are in a spiritual renaissance. As human beings we still have a long road ahead of us. However I do believe it is a core step forward in our journey to have the internet. Spiritually speaking we are making progress because access to various beliefs is so much easier. I do not think it endangers religions as a whole or is something to fear as an organizational institution. Finding Spiritual Well-Being is core to any individual's life and people can find that much easier with the resources at hand. As mentioned before, one can easily research the teachings and beauty of each individual religion and find what speaks to them.

For a rare group of individuals that is found under a name most people associate with entertainment. Whether the study of Vulcan ideology from Star Trek or the study of Jedi ideology from Star Wars, it is all about finding a path and belief which speaks to the individual. Allowing them to grow and live a productive and beneficial life within our world. Service to Others, Responsibility, Integrity, Objectivity, Accountability, Equality, if these are traits being endorsed and passed on, does it matter where the inspiration comes from?

Sorting Fact from Fiction

Fiction reveals truth that reality obscures. ~ Ralph Waldo Emerson

It cannot be denied, Star Wars is fiction. That comes as a major surprise I am sure. Yet what may in fact surprise you is the amount of people who do come looking for the fictional elements. Lightsabers, Force Powers, Battling Evil Lords, and even Immortality. Even when I first started on the Jedi Path I was hoping and asking about real lightsabers. I mean come on, how cool would that be? Ignoring the incredible danger of such a thing of course. Getting back on track. The Star Wars saga ignited the imagination of many and the Jedi took the forefront with their laser-swords and magic-like abilities. Certainly they were concepts which people felt would be infinitely cool to have. I know I wouldn't pass on a chance to own a lightsaber. Again, dangers aside.

So where does one draw the line between fiction and reality? To dismiss Star Wars as completely fictional is simply incorrect. Certainly we can see, especially in retrospect, the spiritual and ethical undertones presented throughout the Star Wars universe. Real and valid ideals which can be compared to various beliefs which already exist. Peace, knowledge, proper use of power, an idea that we are more than our physical shell. So there is an issue of sorting through the material and finding what applies to us in our everyday lives and what does not.

Mostly this comes down to simple common sense and a little research. Are lightsabers real? The short answer is no, at least not on the premise which they are shown in Star Wars. We simply do not have the technology to replicate all of the properties of the lightsaber. Looking at a longer answer, certainly many have sought to create lightsabers. There have been various attempts and many ideas, but ultimately no lightsaber. The MVT

– Metal Vapor Torch has the wow-factor and offers something useful to the right people. Though it is different, it is not a laser, no sword capabilities, something simply designed to burn through tough material such as steel. A potentially great tool for first responders, but not a lightsaber. Wicked Lasers will tell you they have the real deal in their LaserSaber. Which it certainly does have a high-powered laser (spyder 3 lasers 250 mW to 1W), they still require a polycarbonate tube to contain the "blade". It is a much brighter, much more accurate lightsaber replica and also much more dangerous. For price and safety the Force FX Lightsaber toys would be much more advisable in my opinion. Point being, that ultimately the same conclusion is reached. Lightsabers as seen in Star Wars are currently not possible. This shows a simple process of elimination. It is not hard to verify this information with a quick google search these days. Physics.org has a lovely write-up on the scientific issues facing the creation of an actual lightsaber, such as blade containment.

So we can easily rule out a lot of the technology. Spaceships, lightsabers, as cool as these things may be, they are not in our wheel house at the moment. They may ignite the imagination and inspire us to dream, but they do nothing for us in our daily lives. This type of ease in relevance applies the other way as well. In the movie *The Empire Strikes Back* the character Jedi Master Yoda imparts the advice to Luke Skywalker to, be calm, at peace, passive, and allow the answers to come to him. It has a distinctive eastern philosophy vibe. If we look to beliefs like Zen Buddhism we do see a focus on acceptance, on patience, on inner peace and calm. There is a core belief that these elements help one live a less stressful and more productive life. Patience, being at peace, we have known these elements to not only help us in situations, but others have expressed the same sentiments. The value of these concepts is a rather known quantity. We find it is easier to make more objective and rational choices when we are in a state of relaxation than when flustered and full of emotion. Again we can find several sources on the wonderful information super-highway which endorse this viewpoint. Neuroscience is beginning to research these centuries old claims, with preliminary results supporting the concept. Dr. Gaëlle Desbordes has some contributions including a great lecture from February 2011 on the subject (paper available online at isites.harvard.edu) and an ongoing research study (with a research paper published in November 2012 on frontiersin.org). In the end, like lightsabers, our initial hypothesis finds traction in reality. Unlike lightsabers, we find this is something we can live by daily to a positive effect.

In the same movie we see Luke Skywalker running and jumping through the swamps, which presents to us another topic for consideration, physical fitness in relation to the Jedi. Physical well-being is considered a core part of the Jedi lifestyle. Though we must consider two elements just as we did above. Is it conveyed as a core element fictionally and if so is it something we can live by daily with positive and beneficial results? When looking at the overall Star Wars universe physical fitness is a predominate factor for the Jedi. Doesn't matter the era, original trilogy, prequels, expanded universe books, all support Jedi living an active lifestyle which requires and encourages them to stay physically fit. In the prequels we saw a very physical fight between the characters, Obi-Wan Kenobi, Qui-Gon Jinn, and Darth Maul. We also witnessed Yoda jumping around like a pinball in a physical confrontation. In the trilogy, as stated, we saw Luke's training required physical fitness and this being tested both in The Empire Strikes Back and Return of the Jedi. So there is certainly a focus on physicality. The question now becomes is this a beneficial trait to emulate? Certainly, living a healthy and active lifestyle is something we know well improves the quality of our life. Moderation is of course key. Understanding that everyone has a different level of fitness and what is physically healthy for one may not be so for another. My daily work-outs could have an adverse effect on others because I tend to enjoy high-intensity, high-impact work-outs. You have to know your level of fitness and work forward from there. It is not about being a super-model or bodybuilder, but simply living and maintaining a healthy and active lifestyle. Again a rather known and accepted element within our world today.

What proves more elusive is the concept of Force Powers. When it comes to the idea of the Force things start to get a bit more foggy. It is no longer as clear cut as the effects of meditation and physical fitness on the body. These things are measurable and allow us to come to a reasonable conclusion with the scientific method (Question, Hypothesis, Prediction, and Testing, in the most simplistic terms). Technology is easily quantifiable and provides us with a rather quick answer on applicable or not. The Force is a whole other subject. We begin our decent into the world of metaphysics and individual belief in the unknown. We find many labels offering very comparable definitions with no one answer *proving* more correct than any other. So where does the Force fall within our search for real Jedi? Is it a core part of the Jedi within Star Wars? Undeniably. It is in nearly every Star Wars media available. Is it a positive and beneficial concept to live our lives by? The answer would greatly depend on how you define the Force. So instead of devolving into a philosophical questioning of ideas and what names truly mean, lets alter the question slightly. Lets take it in two different directions. The Force as an overall concept and Force Powers.

The Force as an overall concept is a rather intriguing subject. It can fall within any wheelhouse of any religion or philosophy. Call it the Tao, call it the Noosphere, call it the Holy Spirit, call it Qi(chi), the list can go on. Pick a metaphysical concept, pick a religious deity, one can find comparable ideals. If we generalize the concept we can state that spirituality or spiritual well-being was important to the fictional Jedi. Having a firm grasp on your belief system and how that interacted with your life as a Jedi. This is something we can support in our own lives as well. Being firm in our beliefs and being able to address our own spiritual beliefs in relation to being a Jedi is a core element. Whether you fall under the label of Agnostic, Christian, or Buddhist, what matters is finding your own spiritual well-being. People who have a solid spiritual side are hard to fluster regardless of what belief it is. As a Jedi we encourage people to explore their spirituality and find firm footing upon it. Some people find that footing solely in the terminology and definitions of the Force as presented by Star Wars. Certainly George Lucas was inspired by enough real world ideals that such a view does hold its own.

The concept of Force Powers presents a slightly different question. Certainly we can recognize the use and necessity of Force Powers within the Star Wars universe. The question becomes are they positive and beneficial to us as Jedi in our everyday lives? I have met several Jedi. I have gone to yearly gatherings of Jedi from all over the globe. I have lived with Jedi, met them one-on-one, and yet I have not seen anything which could be classified as a Force Power. I feel this ultimately alters the question. Is the pursuit of Force Powers a positive and beneficial endeavor in our everyday lives? If we suspend belief for a second and imagination Force Powers as seen in Star Wars are in fact real, is there a benefit? Sure. The ability to lift heavy objects with your mind would be an invaluable trait. Various search and rescue operations would find such abilities useful. So if they are possible there is certainly an upside to consider. Yet the practice necessary would be involved and take up a good portion of your time. So again we come back to the question being altered. Is there anything as equally or more beneficial you could be doing with that time? Volunteering at a Boys and Girls Club perhaps? Picking up litter at a local park? Feeding the Homeless? Volunteering at an Animal Shelter? Writing a book on a philosophical lifestyle choice? Alright that last one may be questionable, but I think the point is clear. You can spend an hour a day seeking to move a pencil across a table without touching it or you can spend an hour a day doing something nice for someone else. Technically speaking this is left to the individual to decide for themselves. There is no specific Jedi stance that lists service above metaphysical exploration. Likewise a Jedi, like anyone in the world, is free to use their time as they see fit. One can easily argue that spending an hour a day trying to move a pencil is better than an hour of playing a video game. How do you feel your downtime is best spent?

There is no one answer when it comes to the Force. It is an integral part of Jedi lore. It is something that inspires us to question the world around us and seek answers. It is an element of the Jedi ideal that cannot be ignored. However, it is simply an ineffable subject with no single viewpoint reigning supreme. How one pursues it is very much left to the individual. We have come to embrace this diversity and see the value it has. It allows us to share openly our various experiences and interpretations. As a group we have found the benefit in allowing a wide variety of views. It adds flavor to our community, it allows us to compare notes, and fill concept-holes which another viewpoint may miss. There is a strength in our individualistic approach because we continue to study the subject as a group. Something which we will explore as we touch on the subject later on.

An Example of Sorting Fact from Fiction:

Before moving forward I want to highlight the process we have used in exploring our fictional inspiration. The best way to do this is simply show an example of how we approach a specific ideal. For this exercise we'll use an ideal from the fictional Jedi Rules of Behavior created for the Star Wars tabletop role-playing game. We will look at the Jedi concept of "Practice Honesty." We have to recognize the fictional layout and than examine how that actually imparts in our own lives.

The Power of the Jedi sourcebook explains honesty in the Jedi's life as follows:
Honesty is the first responsibility of the Jedi. A Jedi can allow others to believe incorrectly, lead others to incorrect conclusions by playing on their suppositions, or stretch the truth if the situation demands it. A Jedi must always be honest with herself, her Master, and the Council. The Caamasi Jedi Knight Surenit Kil'qiy spoke wisely when he said: "Let there be truth between your heart and the Force. All else is transitory." A Jedi who is honest with her beliefs and her motives finds responsibility to be almost second nature.

This actually presents a pretty clear guideline to follow. It is doesn't require us to judge whether or not it can be applied to everyday life. All of us can easily follow the concept presented. The question is one we should be familiar with by now - is it a positive and beneficial way to live?

The quick and easy answer is yes. Honesty is the best policy after-all, right? Yet when we stop and think many people use white lies all the time. Is it really beneficial to take a strict stance on honesty. If we are asked our opinion on something such as a child's drawing or a spouse's outfit do we simply offer the truth and hope for the best? When our boss asks why we are late, do we say because we were having an intimate moment with the person we love and decided to be late? Being strictly honest carries weight and there can be negative repercussions to giving our honest opinion. So how can we incorporate this ideal which seems core to the Jedi lifestyle and ensure it is a productive part of our lives? We have no desire to alienate people in our lives simply because we value honesty. There must be a middle ground.

First we look at the ideal given and see there is a specific mention of self-honesty. This is absolutely vital to growing as an individual. If you are unable to be honest with yourself, you will have a very difficult time progressing and improving as a person. The Jedi Path does have a focus on self-betterment and on becoming a complete person. So before we jump into the murky of water of when honesty is important we must realize the first step is honesty with ourselves. How can we be honest with others if we won't even recognize the truth within ourselves? We can determine then that being a Jedi requires self-honesty which proves beneficial to our growth.

We recognize that it is better to be honest because it builds trust. Some people may have a tough time with accepting an honest opinion, but they can respect such a person more than someone who lies. The key in this concept lays not with the idea of honesty, but in how it is delivered. Honesty is the best policy, but temper it with understanding and tact. If your spouse asks if the pants make them look fat, you do not respond with, "it is not the pants." Honest? Maybe. Tactful and understanding? No. This is also an area that helps show what might be meant by Jedi being allowed to misdirect people. "I think you look great." It is an honest opinion, though it doesn't really answer the question. If asked about a child's drawing, you can say your honest opinion on how you like colors used. It is a bit of a misdirection giving positive feedback without stating your full opinion. It becomes a question of what is helpful within the situation.

Sometimes tough love is necessary. Strict honesty is something which can prove infinitely more useful to a person than simple platitudes. Part of being a friend to someone is caring enough to tell them the truth. It is great to be encouraging and to provide positive feedback, but do we really grow if we are simply patted on the head when our work can be much better? This is the consideration and balancing act placed upon Jedi. We come to the conclusion that as a Jedi it is better to live an honest life than to deny our responsibilities.

This ideal was not placed upon the Jedi by a fictional source. That is what brought it to our attention, but what placed it upon us as a group was the simple fact that it is a positive way to live. That Jedi who have lived by and tested this ideal have found it to be a beneficial way to conduct their lives. They have come to understand the balancing act needed, but certainly find that it is a worthwhile pursuit. All Jedi really embrace the concept of self-honesty as well. When we are able to acknowledge our actions openly, we can accept the responsibility for our successes and our mistakes much more freely. Every Jedi can give you plenty of personal examples of living by this ideal. No matter what Jedi group you venture to, you will find a focus on honesty and self-knowledge. Time and again Jedi have looked at this fictional concept and found it to be a valuable tool in the Jedi toolbox. We are inspired by the fiction, but it must prove productive in our daily lives for it to find a home in our core philosophy.

This is a simple example of using the basics of the scientific method as we progress and define the Jedi Path. First the question, is this fictional Jedi ideal a beneficial and positive way to live one's life? Then we make a hypothesis based upon previous life experience, knowledge of fictional Jedi experiences, and a basic understanding of how the world works (societal values, physics, history, etc.). From this examination, usually involving other Jedi, we come to a prediction. A logical deduction base upon our various knowledge and what we believe will transpire. Lastly, we must verify this by testing the theory. That is tested through various people and retested continually. This is why the pursuit of Force Powers has taken a backseat in the Jedi Community. Over the past decade we have seen time and again that using our time on service projects yields more positive results than sitting in our rooms trying to master the Force. It is a process that we have followed for years for even the most simplistic concepts. It is also why I often make the mistake of leaving things unsaid or invalidated, because I take for granted the time, effort, and experience put into the ideas and simply feel they speak for themselves. Here is to hoping I curb that bad habit for this book.

Jedi as a Religion

Movies can and do have tremendous influence in shaping young lives in the realm of entertainment towards the ideals and objectives of normal adulthood. ~ Walt Disney

 Before we get into the meat and potatoes of Jedi ideals I need to take a moment and speak on the viability of the Jedi being an actual religion. It is my hope to strengthen the position of the Jedi as a personal religion. It is my goal to enforce the position of someone claiming the Jedi as their religion. It requires a re-examining of what we define and label a religion as. We have to confront how society generally defines a religious group and show the validity behind calling the Jedi your religion despite the arguments against it which can be made.
 This is a bit tough to touch on because individual views on the word religion differ greatly. We will look at the textbook definition of the word, but we will also look at the more common standards people hold to religious institutions. In 2001 when the Jedi religion reached world-wide media attention I was a voice against it. Religion just carries a lot of negative connotations for myself. I also dislike being compared to the cults that claim religious status trying to prove validity. For me it brought ideas of organizational oversight from unqualified people to an already fluid, diverse, and useful path. The idea that some teenage fanboy was going to have the right to tell me what defined and made a Jedi was not something I endorsed. Pot calling the kettle black a bit, I know. Regardless I fought against the idea of Jedi as a religion. I simply didn't see the need for such. A philosophy, a lifestyle, an ethical outlook on how one conducts and approaches life, all of these I agreed with, but religion? I just couldn't sink my teeth into it. So I have argued against the Jedi Religion for nearly a decade. It provides me with a unique perspective to approach this from. I am sure my conclusion of the Jedi as a religion might

surprise some people.

The Jedi Religion:
Rivers, ponds, lakes and streams - they all have different names, but they all contain water. Just as religions do - they all contain truths. ~ Muhammad Ali

The word religion often brings certain images to mind. For me those are people gathered in a building, sitting in reverence, and praying to a God. A person standing up in front of people delivering a viewpoint on faith as if it were concrete truth. For me I see religion as stagnation. It claims truth and thus does not question and grow with the world around it. I think this is more evident now than ever before. Major religions in the world have to contend with the evolving acceptance of diversity. Personally I see open-minded exploration of new ideas winning out. I talk with more and more Christians denouncing the teachings of Leviticus and feel the message of compassion and acceptance of all God's creatures is the proper direction to be moving. So the idea that an open and evolving path, which had been helping me through a tough time in life, being turned into a religion was not something I was willing to accept. So I spoke out and found some interesting points to tackle.

What are the major defining factors of a religion? Dictionary definition aside, what defines a religion as an organization? Well there are core ideas and practices which typically accompany all religions. There is a standard and overall accepted belief in an afterlife, what happens when you die. There is an accepted belief in the creation of world/universe, such as how and who created it. There is some supernatural body which is involved in the previous two concepts, usually a deity of some kind. There is an accepted form of worship of said deity. An accepted and established place of worship, e.g. a church. As I mentioned before, I had concerns of an Ecclesiastical Government being put into place. I also worried about open membership; if Jedi is a religion does that mean one cannot be a

Jedi and a Christian (for example)? Generally religions do not allow that cross-over, you are either one or the other. These points tend to make the Jedi as less of a religious organization and more of a spiritual guide in religious matters.

So there was and is a need to tackle some of these concerns in an organized manner. We need to explore the validity of this claim of religious status. How close does the Jedi come to being a religion with the points listed above?

Creation, Prayers, and Councils:

The concept of an afterlife, creation of the universe, and an associated deity can all be tackled with the same resounding truth in the Jedi Community: It is left up to the individual to decide. A specific Jedi group may put into stone a belief in a supernatural concept. They can tell you that the Force created the universe and that your energy returns to the Force when you die. But what if you chose not to believe that? Simple fact is, if you disagree with that it does not make you any less of a Jedi. If you hold to a Wiccan view of energies and deities and what happens when you die, you can still be a Jedi. You may need to find a new Jedi group, but you can still be a Jedi. Your specific and individual belief in the creation of the universe, in the afterlife, in a deity does not affect your ability to live as a Jedi. It is not a requirement to be a Jedi. The only major requirement Jedi have overall is that you do work on your spiritual well-being. That you do explore the big questions and find a conclusion that works for you and gels with your outlook in life.

To be a Jedi there is no required definition of the Force that you must swallow. You can view the Force as a natural energy source. You can view it as the residual energy of kinetic and thermal energy being created and released on a daily basis. You can seek a more biological view of mitochondria mirroring the fictional concept presented in the prequel movies of Star Wars. You can have a view that the Force is another word for the Gods or God you believe in. You can have the view that the Force is simply the natural human abilities we all possess. That our five senses work in ways we are not fully aware of and at times that can make it seem like we have a sixth sense. It does not truly matter how one approaches the subject of the Force. Simply that they do so with an open-mind and willingness to explore a plethora of possibilities. This separates the Jedi from most major religions in my opinion. There isn't a claim to truth, there is simply individual exploration supported by like-minded seekers. Does this mean the Jedi cannot be a religion? Perhaps in the traditional sense that we have come to know it. Or perhaps it is just a change in how we are looking, and will look, at religious beliefs. An acceptance of personal beliefs without judgment and condemnation.

  Another well-recognized part of a religious organization is a founded place of worship. Churches, Temples, Sacred Ground, groups typically meet in a very specific location to share their devotion. Some Jedi groups have worked hard to ensure this type of atmosphere for their members. Others have a strictly online presence when it comes to this concept. While other Jedi groups do not hold to the concept at all. Like before it is a varied and non-committal practice which varies and changes depending on who you are and what group you are with. The Temple of the Jedi Order does have a weekly meeting in-person. The Jedi Church did meet regularly at a Catholic church. It is an important practice for some groups. Yet it is not a mandatory part of living as a Jedi.

  If one considers the time needed in the online environment this changes a bit. The Jedi connect to people all over the world via the internet. It is what has allowed the community to not only survive, but thrive. Sharing and studying Jedi ideals, practices, and personal experiences is a necessary part of the learning process. This mainly takes place online. One can easily state this interactive involvement is the virtual equivalent to a church or temple atmosphere. A place where one studies, discusses, and explores the concepts of the Jedi Path. It requires continual involvement and most groups have a weekly structure plan one can follow for those interested. We can see how the Jedi don't quite fit the mold of an organized religion in the known sense, but certainly there are comparisons which do measure up. The major difference here is that not all Jedi sites would fall under the terminology of worship. Rather it is educational study more than praising any deity or supernatural force. Does this mean the Jedi is not a religion? I still say it falls to approaching it with a wider lens than what we have come to accept as a normal religious institution.

Ecclesiastical Government is an easy issue to tackle. Jedi have no singular authority which rules the community. Something I am extremely thankful and grateful for. Having a Vatican-type system for the Jedi is not something I feel meshes well with our diverse and open style. Each group however does have a organizational structure of authority. In the movies the Jedi had the Jedi Council which might fall under the definition of a Ecclesiastical Government. In reality we have administration teams that help organize and manage the individual web-groups. The Jedi Academy Online has a small administration team of four members who address the progress, issues, and educational needs of the group. They determine the work and direction of the JAO internet-organization. Each group has its own style and structure which allows it to function in a way they approve of. This is closer to how a charity might be set-up than any sort of religious institution. The Jedi do not have an avatar they look to as embodying the entirety of their path. There is no one council which directly affects all Jedi groups. I personally don't feel it is necessary for religious or spiritual advancement. It may be a commonalty in major religions, but I am not sure it is a necessary element for claiming to be a religion.

The Jedi do not have a bible. Not even Star Wars has the direct influence it once did. As shown in the previous section, as Jedi we look to sort fact from fiction. There is no one document in the Jedi Community that all Jedi conform too. There is no scared text which all Jedi are beholden too. There are a few that have come close. The fictional Jedi Code is widely explored by the Jedi. The Jedi Circle is something that resonates with many Jedi and has been shared amongst a lot of Jedi groups. There is simply a shared group of practices and ideals which define the Jedi as Jedi. These are found in a plethora documents and websites. Because of this, there is no set doctrine on how one becomes a Jedi. Each group has their own way of helping a person find their own way on the Jedi Path. One might use that as a reason against religion. I find it allows the open atmosphere that defines the Jedi Community. Where a Christian might find it hard to also be a Wiccan especially with the Ten Commandments having God stating no other deities and idols before Him. The Jedi do not have any such restrictions on cross-faith or cross-religious beliefs. Many find the Jedi to be perfectly supplemental, encouraging them to be better Taoists (for example). Some find the opposite, that their faith makes them excel within the Jedi Path. Either way Jedi find their path is beneficial and allows a person to find the complete version of themselves.

The Dictionary Says:
There are five entries listed under dictionary.com's definition of the word religion. We'll tackle each one to determine a more textbook viewpoint of whether or not Jedi can be classified as a religion. The first one is the longest and most accepted definition of the word. *"A set of beliefs concerning the cause, nature, and purpose of the universe, especially when considered as the creation of a superhuman agency or agencies, usually involving devotional and ritual observances, and often containing a moral code governing the conduct of human affairs."* This has somewhat been covered by our previous look at the word. I still want to take each point in turn briefly though.

Cause, nature, and purpose of the universe tends to fall under the personal belief section of the Jedi. As a group, as a community, there is no singular viewpoint which prevails. There is no universal goal which all life is meant to fulfill supported by the Jedi as a whole. The nature of the universe finds itself explained in a variety of ways within the Jedi Community. While one can make an argument for their group's view or their personal view, as a community we are very diversified in this area.

The second entry is a more Jedi friendly concept. *"A specific fundamental set of beliefs and practices generally agreed upon by a number of persons or sects: the Christian religion; the Buddhist religion."* This one we can say definitely applies to the Jedi community as a whole. Those fundamental beliefs and practices are documented in this book. They are seen in the Jedi Code and the Jedi Circle. There is definitely a core to the Jedi belief that transcends the various Jedi groups.

Even if one simply distilled it down to belief in Peace, Knowledge, Serenity, Harmony, and the Force. Or a focus on personal improvement in the areas of physical, mental, spiritual, emotional, social, environmental, and financial well-being. There is definitely a core message which is found throughout the Jedi Community. So certainly I feel we can say this definition of the word religion can be applied to the Jedi.

The third entry, *"the body of persons adhering to a particular set of beliefs and practices: a world council of religions"* is really just a repeat of the previous. However this also acknowledges the individual groups as a religion. This one can apply more to the tribal web-group structure of the Jedi Community. Certain Jedi Religion sites have a specific belief structure in place. They teach about the Force in a very specific way which they fully believe to be self-evident. Not all groups agree, but this definition certainly endorses the individualistic views which exist.

The fourth entry is a bit vague for my tastes. *"The life or state of a monk, nun, etc.: to enter religion."* Certainly the fictional Jedi had a monastic lifestyle, but we do not. That said certainly one can make the case that the life or state of being a Jedi does qualify. We have daily practices we adhere too. We have a specific way in which we conduct our lives. We do have a code of ethics to which we adhere. So certainly this definition can be applied to the Jedi as a whole. One could say anyone truly living as a Jedi does so in a religious sense. They do live the life of a Jedi.

The final entry doesn't offer a final resolution. *"The*

practice of religious beliefs; ritual observance of faith." Some Jedi sites adhere to this. Some Jedi groups do not fall under this. As a whole, this would be difficult to apply to the Jedi specifically. This brings us full circle to the individualistic concept which applies to our community. The Jedi simply do not have a community-wide practice of specific religious beliefs.

My Jedi Religion:
The world is my country, all mankind are my brethren, and to do good is my religion. ~ Thomas Paine

There is a Jedi by the name of Andy Spalding who presented one of the best arguments for the Jedi as a Religion. We were sitting on the couch and he presented it in this format: Working out is my prayers. Service is my gospel. The world is my church. - For me this stuck because it was an angle I had planned on taking for this section. Originally the title was going to be Jedi as Religion, but this is more accurately to the reality. Jedi as My Religion. Those that follow the Jedi Religion do so because it is a scared and holy act to them in how they live. Service to others being the highest form of worship they can offer. Physical fitness being a form of reverence. This is where people dub themselves Jediists.

This is also why many could make a successful argument for myself to be following the Jedi Religion. A Christian isn't just about belief, they will tell you it is in how they live their lives. As the bible verse goes, Faith without works is dead. Likewise for the Jedi it isn't about a specific deity, but in how one lives and conduct themselves in their daily life. It is here, in this reasoning, that most find their home under the Jedi Religion label. The Jedi have a set of core practices, beliefs, and ethics. Jedi have specific goals they seek to accomplish. They have certain practices which could be spun as rituals which we seek to fulfill everyday. Meditation, physical fitness, helping others, seeking peace and harmony with the world around us. Concepts and ideals we strive towards as a singular group.

To use a quote from the movie Dogma, *"It doesn't matter what you believe, as long as you believe something."* - Metatron. Or perhaps Serenity, *"I don't care what you believe in, just believe in it."* - Shepard Book. When you live something day-in and day-out it becomes your religion. People have said in all seriousness that football is their religion. Why? Because it is what they pay reverence too. It is what they live by, it is what guides their decision-making. Jedi have reported having profound experiences in the midst of their daily practices. That they have felt something greater and larger than themselves simply by living as a Jedi. They have felt their lives impacted and changed simply by completing the five goals of the Jedi. As such I would say that qualifies the Jedi for the religious label.

Conclusion:

Is the Jedi an official religion? Does it matter? If we are to try and stack up the Jedi as a religion against the centuries old religious institutions than the answer is no. The Jedi obviously fall way short in several categories. One can argue age, the Jedi is almost twenty years old, but I ask is that the point of religion? To be like the other guy? Is that truly the defining factor? Whether or not you are similar to other belief systems out there? Whether or not you hold worship in a specific way on a certain day? I am not convinced that standard of defining religion is the proper and right way to go. I do not believe that is what makes a religion.

Instead my conclusion falls to the individual. Is it your religion? Is it what you wish to follow as a religious practice? Then everything else is irrelevant. I personally don't bother with such labels. Lifestyle, philosophy, religion, all takes a back seat to the question of beneficial and positive living in my opinion. If one labels it their religion I feel there is enough to warrant that viewpoint. And certainly they should enjoy the same religious freedoms as anyone else. By looking at the dictionary there is enough to points to be made for the Jedi as religion. Which is probably why some Jedi groups have succeeded in obtaining non-profit religious group tax status. That and as mentioned, as individual groups they can definitively state an accepted viewpoint on the Force and religious practices.

My issue is that people feel if the Jedi are viewed and recognized as an official religion it will validate their path in life. That is a sad outlook in my opinion. No Jedi, heck no person should require the approval of others. Whether the world accepts the Jedi as a religion or not should never stop you or anyone from believing in what you want to believe in. It should never stop you from living a lifestyle you find productive and useful in your own life. Validation of the Jedi Path is proven within itself. It is found within the experience, tested and proven with time.

I don't know if the Jedi will ever reach any sort of accepted state in the world. What I do know is that it will not affect me either way and I doubt it would affect any Jedi. We will continue to live our lives by the Jedi ideals. I will still wake-up tomorrow and follow the Jedi practices regardless of the general consensus on my belief system. I will still write, teach, and ramble about the Jedi ideology regardless of acceptance. Though I suppose that this is a bit fluffy for a book specifically entitled the Jedi Religion. Still that is my conclusion. Just like the Jedi as a Religion you can take it or leave it.

IDEALS

To have striven, to have made the effort, to have been true to certain ideals - this alone is worth the struggle. ~ William Osler

As mentioned there are core ideals which all Jedi follow. These cross websites, categories, and labels. Some places expand beyond these ideals and include other concepts, but these are things all Jedi follow. Since 1995 Jedi online have been looking to define themselves outside of comparisons to preexisting paths. We looked at the fiction and took from Star Wars the basic ideals expressed. This generally is found in the form of the Jedi Code. The Jedi Code was written for the West End Games Star Wars Tabletop Role-Playing Guide in 1987. It was a simple four line code which reads as follows:

There is no emotion; there is peace.
There is no ignorance; there is knowledge.
There is no passion; there is serenity.
There is no death; there is the Force.

The Jedi Code has been expanded upon and changed throughout the fiction. Likewise in the online environment several people have sought to write a better version. One of those attempts resulted in the Jedi Circle. The Jedi Circle ended up simply condensing these to the base ideals – Peace, Knowledge, Serenity, Harmony, and the Force. Drawing upon the five line Jedi Code which came about in 1996. While the Jedi Circle gained popularity and notoriety within the Jedi Community it went beyond basic ideology. It covers a more broad definition of the simplistic foundation of the Jedi Path. Including practices, traits, and misconceptions, which go beyond what we are looking to examine here.

Instead of simply offering an examination of the Jedi Code or using the Jedi Circle I will be listing certain core ideals which all Jedi share. I do this for a couple of reasons. First reason, books already exist which cover the Jedi Circle and the Jedi Code in a more in-depth manner. To reiterate that information would not only be unjust to the subject matter, but unfair to those who already own those books as well. The second reason is because the ideals I have chosen are too often taken for granted by the Jedi. They are sort of no-brainers to Jedi. Ideals that tend go without saying and because of that they rarely get the attention they deserve. We, as Jedi, can forget at times that just because we live it daily doesn't mean it is evident to the common observer.

Now we will be covering these staples of Jedi ideology one at a time in a very basic manner. Allow me to say this; if you are looking for a deeper exploration into the Jedi ideals, goals, and practices, please seek out a Jedi group. You can find that information in the last section of this book. This isn't even going to be an elementary look at these concepts. Simply an overview of these concepts. I know Jedi working on entire books dedicated to a singular ideal. Covering the full spectrum of responsibility that a Jedi has is a very deep subject. This applies to all the ideals listed below. So this is simply to offer an overview of the shared ideals Jedi have.

The Best You Possible:
Try to be like the turtle - at ease in your own shell. ~ Bill Copeland

Jedi training is called such because it is a time of preparation and testing for the self. The main ideal behind becoming a Jedi is becoming the best version of You. It is one thing to want to help others, it is quite another to be able to help others. George R. Price is a great example of this principle. An idea that in order to help people you must be in a position to help people. Else it will simply end badly for all involved.

The Jedi ideals are rooted in service to others. They are concepts of living for the world around us. Some seek to accomplish this by involving themselves in search-and-rescue. Some accomplish this by feeding the homeless, giving to children in need, it is a very long list. These things should not be done at the expense of your own life. They should be done because you can do them and the fact you can do them without hurting yourself in any way (financial, physical, emotional, etc.).

The Jedi Path seeks world-betterment. This is simply undeniable focus of our path. Within Star Wars fiction Jedi often took active interest in the galaxy and planets they lived on. They weren't police officers of the galaxy. They simply were capable individuals who recognized that because they had the ability to help, they had the responsibility to help. When to help, how to help, and determining when it is best stand back comes with that responsibility, but is a subject for another time. The concept here is a simple one. You want to help the world? Learn to help yourself first. Otherwise you are just building on sand.

So the question becomes how does one become the best version of themselves possible? It starts with the self. Self-honesty, knowledge of the self, self-reflection. We have to confront and eventually be able to accept who we are within this moment. That may be something that makes a person feel good. It could be something that makes one feel depressed. The thing to remember is that we are not bound by who we are now. You don't like it? Change it. It is possible, it is not outside the realm of reality. I had to face my own demons and confront the person I was. It is the first step – accepting who we are, embracing that, and than choosing to move forward. Feeding some traits more than others and building ourselves into the image we want to be.

For the Jedi we can a complete approach. We use meditation, physical fitness, philosophical and ethical studies. We focus on several areas of personal well-being to truly determine where we are at and where we want to be. Then we practice traits such as patience and objectivity as we go through the process of self-improvement. It can be a tough and tedious process. It can be a scary and heavy journey to take, but one that proves invaluable when you come out the other side.

No Jedi's journey is exactly the same. As noted throughout this book we embrace diversity. A meditation that worked wonders for one Jedi may prove useless for another. The core is the same however, continually working towards becoming the best version of us possible. We often need help in this journey. Whether that be from family, friends, or professionals such as doctors. They help us navigate the various obstacles we face in striving for self-improvement.

Physical Well-Being:
The method for health promotion is based on water, as flowing water never grows stale. The idea is not to overdevelop or to overexert, but to normalize the function of the body. ~ Bruce Lee

    Six pack abs and rock hard pecs. No. That is not what we are talking about when we say physical well-being. First note, everyone's level of physical well-being differs. Some of us have medical problems which limit what exactly our wellness is. But lets keep that within reason. A bum knee is no excuse to be out of shape. You have plenty of ways to keep active, even with medical conditions. Which any hospital rehab center will prove. The idea here is not to grow stagnate.
    This is about finding your personal physical health. It is about staying active, keeping a thought towards eating right, and all that fun jazz. Our physical health does play a part in how we feel, in our emotional well-being. We want to build and encourage a healthy lifestyle. That doesn't mean looking like a Calvin Klein model nor does it mean running like Usain Bolt. You don't have to lose the fast food all together, but certainly moderation is key.
    That is the jest of what we are talking about here. Moderation. For some people, they are fit, they are model-like, they may have a vegan diet. That works for them. It is what they want and what helps them stay healthy. For others it is simply getting in the daily hour basketball session with the locals. Cutting down on the fast food intake and taking the stairs at work works for others. Some Jedi run in marathons, some in obstacle races, that is their level of fitness and health. It is what they enjoy and helps keep them moving. Others have to use a stationary bike,

a swimming pool, or Pilates. Not everyone is a runner, but running is far from the only way to stay active.

When I was going through a rough time in my life my physical health suffered as a result. As such all my areas of well-being were out of whack. One of the main things that helped me get back into the swing of things was running in Spartan Races. These are obstacle mud runs. Fun stuff in my opinion. As a Jedi I knew physical well-being played a core part in my mental and emotional health. So I decided to participate. It changed me around. I was excited to work-out. I loved the challenges. That dedication to my physical fitness really spurred a complete 180 in my life. The physical is the foundation to build from. It can inspire, encourage, and help lift you to sunny places.

As we mentioned before we see Luke training in the swamps of Dagobah. He is training physically along with his other practices. Life is made of activity. The energy to approach life head-on can be cultivated and grown. You can build your reserves and expand your strength to tackle the world. Again, this isn't about a muscle-man lifestyle. It is about staying fit and healthy for you. It is about being active and not falling into a rut of stagnation.

This is one of those mixed concepts. Physical health is about working within your abilities. If you hurt yourself trying to run a triathlon when your doctor said your knee won't hold? That is not being healthy. That is maintaining your physical well-being. The human body's natural state is not a chiseled six pack stomach. There is a reason people work really hard to get them and keep them. You want to find and maintain your personal health. That includes diet, exercise, and being safe.

The point is a simple one. A 60 year old Jedi and a 21 year old Jedi are not going to have the same physical fitness level. They will not have the same health needs or focuses. As such their exercises, diet, and activities may be very different. They can both have great physical well-being, but their daily routines may look completely different. We as Jedi encourage one to find their physical wellness and continually work on it. It really does

make a huge difference in one's life.
    Our base ideal here is to encourage constant physical activity. From a daily jog to chasing the kids around the house for an hour (only an hour if you are lucky). We want to build a foundational structure. One of the cornerstones of that foundation is physical well-being. It is simply too important to fully ignore.

Emotional Well-Being:
If your emotional abilities aren't in hand, if you don't have self-awareness, if you are not able to manage your distressing emotions, if you can't have empathy and have effective relationships, then no matter how smart you are, you are not going to get very far. ~ Daniel Goleman

    If there is one aspect that I had to label not just the cornerstone, but the foundational stone of the Jedi, it would have to be Emotional Well-Being. Without Emotional Well-Being everything else crumbles. It all becomes meaningless. It is also one of the biggest focuses of the Jedi, both fictionally speaking and in real life. Some would say emotional control. But that is the first baby step. Ultimately what we are talking about is Emotional Stability. Feeling openly and freely without adverse effect. Where you can feel angry and not have the knee-jerk reaction to punch the wall. Where you can love and not require possession. Goethe is by far my favorite example, *"If I love you, what business is it of yours?"* Words I have come to live by, which really just embody the idea of emotional stability for me.
    For the Jedi emotional stability is what we strive for. It is repeated throughout the fiction. It is repeated throughout our actual lessons. Peace, serenity, harmony. Finding the equilibrium with our emotional state of being. Find the balance between our emotions and are rational state of mind. While the fictional side of things tended to advocate a more stoic sense of being. We have come to embrace the essence of emotional content. Acknowledging, accepting, and embracing our emotions as the guides they are.

Anger is a sign, it is a indicator. Likewise with joy, happiness, and love. These all tell us important things about ourselves and how we interact with the world. What angers us and why reveals a lot about ourselves. It tells us things we hold close and view as important. It is why an action can be meaningless to one person and mean the world to another. It is where a lot of misunderstandings come from. *"I can't understand why a person would act such a way."* I am sure you have heard such or even said it before. First step to understanding starts with the self. We have to understand our own emotional motivations before we start to try and unravel someone else's.

This is an area where I failed horribly at in recent memory. I had ignored my emotional well-being. I bottled things up, I didn't communicate how I felt, and simply ran away from the problems I was facing. As such I found myself way more stressed out than I should have been. I was quick to react emotionally. I was very quick to anger. Eventually I just shut people out. I closed down emotionally and simply disappeared in whatever fictional medium would hold my attention. Now besides this obviously being a not very healthy way to live. It certainly wasn't a fun way to live and something I feel wasted precious moments in life. This proved true when my relationships failed around me and I lost out on those possible memories.

The one thing that really suffered? My desire to help. I had no desire to be of service to others, to help better myself or the world around me. I simply didn't care if other people needed help. All that mattered was my emotional distress. Wasn't looking to resolve it, simply wallow in it. This one element was out of whack and it made the other core elements of the Jedi fall to the wayside. This is simply how it works. Your emotional wellness will determine your motivation to follow through. This counts in your physical fitness, on your service projects, even your social interaction.

So we focus in on emotional well-being. We seek to make peace with ourselves, with our emotions, to come to a fair understanding within. That our emotions are an important part of who we are and how we live within the world. They are not to be feared, controlled, or bottled up. They are to be embraced, they are to be understood. Your actions and decision are born from a harmony of emotion and reason, rationality and emotional intelligence. This is what we are talking about when we mention emotional well-being. Stability and Harmony.

Spiritual Well-Being:
The goal of spiritual practice is full recovery, and the only thing you need to recover from is a fractured sense of self. ~ Marianne Williamson

An automatic by-product of the Force. It is a major theme within the Star Wars saga and an inescapable concept we must address as Jedi. We do this in the form on encouraging spiritual well-being. What do you believe? Why? Does that make sense to you? What about conflicting beliefs? In other words are you secure enough in your beliefs that you allow other people to have differing ones? Spiritual well-being is about securing your beliefs. Securing them for you and no one else. The main thing about our spiritual outlook is that it shapes how we view and interact with the world. It is often a clear indicator of what helps us explain this crazy world we live in.

It is not necessarily about religious belief, but certainly that can be the answer as well. An Atheist can be as spiritually fit as a Christian. A Buddhist can have the same spiritual wellness as someone who is Agnostic. This isn't about your religious title as much as it is about coming to terms with your spiritual beliefs. Are events senseless? Random? Is disease a natural by-product or a creation of a higher power? We want to build a strong sense of spiritual wellness. People who are secure in their spiritual views generally are free to openly explore the various spiritual concepts out there without fear. They don't have to worry about being lead astray or brainwashed.

There are stories of cults having mass-suicides. Horrible events. Yet the people within them were searching for something.

If you have a strong spiritual well-being than no one can use that to lead you to answers you don't fully understand (or perhaps even agree with). It isn't about listening to someone else. It isn't about some outside answer. Spiritual well-being is about finding your answers and being absolutely 100% secure in those answers. They come from within and speak to you on a deeper level. They work for you and that is what counts. It is not about proof or having all the answers. Agnostics do not profess to have the answers, yet they can have great spiritual wellness. It is about finding and defining your beliefs. Understand that those may grow and evolve with time. Just because a person is secure in their spirituality doesn't mean they stop growing. It is usually the opposite. The more secure one is in your their beliefs the more they welcome spiritual exploration.

As we gain experience, knowledge, and understanding our views and beliefs can change with us. Being secure in your spirituality doesn't mean you stagnate believing you have all the answers. It simply means you have found the answers that work for you currently. It means you are solid within your spiritual faith – whatever that may be.

We have touched on this already a bit in discussing Jedi as a Religion. It isn't about defining a Godhead. Or providing you with answers on what happens when we die. We don't profess to know how the universe was created. All of this is for you to question, explore, and explain in your own way. Certainly we encourage such exploration. It is good to have a solid view on the more mysterious aspects of our universe and life. Even if that is simply a 'go with the flow' type of outlook.

God. Afterlife. Fate. Free Will. What are you views? How do you explain the mysteries of the universe? Do you even bother to try? Why or Why Not? Building a solid foundation in this area ultimately extends into other areas as well. Believing things happen for a reason will ultimately play into how you deal with emotional issues. It will affect your ethical outlook. Likewise believing that all things are simply cause and effect will play a part in how you interact with the world around you. So question.

Seek *your* answers. Do not be bound by one idea, if it doesn't work for you. Combine them all if need be.

The Jedi can help in the exploration, but we are not here to provide the answers. No one can tell you what to believe. That is something you must determine on your own for your own reasons. It must be something that comes from within and means something to you. You never have to explain it or justify it if you do not want too. Just believe it and grow with it. That is what we mean with spiritual well-being.

Ethical Well-Being:
A man without ethics is a wild beast loosed upon this world. ~ Albert Camus

What we are talking about with ethical well-being is directly related to decision-making. Integrity, Responsibility, Accountability. The Jedi Ideals are one to encourage and enforce ethical decision-making. We have a specific way of thinking. We do hold to the "good guy" paradigm. Thus in order to ensure that mentality we focus on ethical stability. If you find a bag of 100,000 dollars in it, what do you do? The honest answer is one that benefits the self. Yet the philosophical outlook for the Jedi is one of placing the needs of others before ourselves. There is an addendum to that, but we'll cover in financial well-being.

The point here is to acknowledge and confirm the white hat good guy ideal. Jedi are bound by certain ethical restrictions. The ends do **not** justify the means. *How* a Jedi achieves the outcome is just as important as what that outcome is. Intention, Action(Reaction), and Outcome play an equal role within Jedi thought. If your goal is to help a person grow and become better, but do so at the expense of someone else, is that truly a proper action to take?

The Jedi seek the win-win scenario. It is not always possible, but it is the idea we strive for. Certainly Jedi understand that you have to break some eggs to make an omelet. It is the inevitability of the world we live in. Sacrifices must be made when trying to reach a specific goal. Yet Jedi will always encourage and seek that elusive option that allows everyone to benefit from the situation. Even if said individuals don't always know it or recognize it right away.

While Jedi have ethical restrictions they also have leeway. Jedi are allowed room to act and react within any given situation. We briefly covered this in the honesty exploration in the sorting fact from fiction section. Intention and Action is judged more harshly than the outcome. But as mentioned all three are held to a high standard. Still Jedi are allowed to use subterfuge, they can allow other people to believe their own false assumptions. A Jedi doesn't *have* to speak the truth, they can chose not to answer, or retort with a question in return. All those fun, frustrating, diplomatic tactics, that toe the line.

Understand of course, allowed and encouraged are too different things. Mostly you will find those that follow the Jedi way of life prefer honest and objective communication. They encourage it and live by it. It simplifies a lot in life to simply be open and honest with others. You have to be mindful. You have to apply common sense. If you are continually late to work and tell your boss it is because you were out drinking all the time. Not going to have a job for long. Also will be getting a lot of lectures and extra work form your Jedi mentor. The thing to remember is simple: The Jedi are the good guys. Be Fair, Have Integrity, Take Responsibility.

Ethical well-being is about establishing your ethical guideline throughout life. What you are willing and unwilling to do. The Jedi have their standard and their concept of ethical decision-making, but that still leaves room for personal application. You have to find your path within the ethical limitations of the Jedi. It seems smaller than it truly is, but that is more due to the vague nature in which I am approaching the subject. As an example, there are many ways to diffuse a hostile situation and it is left to each Jedi to come to their own way of doing so.

Ethical well-being with the Jedi starts with our baseline

concepts. Broad concepts of integrity, accountability, and so forth. Each of those offers room for an individual to put their own unique spin on them. The main thing is fully developing and understanding your ethical stance. Being 100% clear about your principles and the lines you simply will not cross no matter what. Like all areas of well-being it requires exploration and questioning. Establish your ethical guideline and live by it, test it, and allow it to grow as needed.

Financial Well-Being:
A big part of financial freedom is having your heart and mind free from worry about the what-ifs of life. ~ Suze Orman

    A simple idea that can be easily misunderstood. No, this is not about being rich. This is about finding your financial well-being. Not some other person's idea of what your yearly salary should be. This is not about money-grubbing. It is a two-part concept. First, understand that you cannot give what you do not have. Simple concept. If you want to help others you have to be in a position to do so. Second part, living comfortably for yourself. Finding what makes you happy and living within that. Being free from worry. Does wonders for your emotional and mental well-being. I'll probably have to expand on these huh?
    Financial responsibility is simply a necessary element to the world we live in. Living within your means and living comfortably within your means. Now for some people that is a trailer and a piece of land; inexpensive, but theirs'. Some people however might find that financial success is the greatest tool to help others. Thus they seek the big paycheck, the fancy house, and do not shy away from the fact they are well off. It is about finding your comfort zone and ensuring you can obtain it. Give me a roof and some internet and I am good. Doesn't take much to accomplish that. Yet if I wanted or felt more comfortable in the big house, I would need to re-focus on finding a career that supported that lifestyle.
    Likewise the ways I seek to help out are rather

inexpensive. I participate in the Big Brother program. That doesn't take a whole lot of money out of my paycheck. I buy the occasional toy for homeless kids, again not a wallet breaker. I use crowdrise (crowdrise.com – use it – love it), again doesn't hurt my finances. These are ways I can give back without going outside my means. Also giving my time online, offering the lessons and support for the Jedi. These are all ways I fulfill my responsibilities as a Jedi which fall within my financial ability to do. You hear of celebrities who donate 25,000 dollars here, 50,000 there. They can afford those invests to give back to the community. They can make a positive impact by investing their money is good charities. But in order to really be able to help in that way, you have to be in the financial position to do so.

    The key for that is simply going after a career and lifestyle that you can agree with. It is about finding a balance between working and giving. You have to provide for yourself first or you'll find that you are the one receiving the help. This is the major essence of financial well-being. It is not about being rich. It is about ensuring that you are capable of helping as you would like. You can do that from your parent's house. You can do that from a rented house boat. You can do it from a twenty-million dollar mansion.

    If you are still in school, have a clear idea of where you'd like to go. What you would like to be. Invest in your future. Be patient with yourself. As a starving college student you may not be able to help the world in the way you want just yet. But work hard, achieve your goals, and when you are 32 you can say how you have changed the world. Find your niche. Be a Zoologist, a Theoretical Physicist, a Elementary School Teacher, whatever your desire may be. Understand the financial freedoms and restraints involved and embrace it. Work within it and find your comfort zone. From there you'll find plenty of opportunities to help out in the world.

    This is the core of financial well-being. Being free from the worry of monetary pressures that society places on us. Seek your dream and live within your means. I would never ask anything more of you. The question is – do you ask more of yourself? If so, get to resolving one of the issues. Either the size of your paycheck or the size of charity check.

Goals

What you get by achieving your goals is not as important as what you become by achieving your goals. ~ Henry David Thoreau

    All Jedi share common goals within our path. We also each have our own individual goals. Whether that is a specific career goal or a house with a white picket fence goal or running a zombie race goal. Jedi organizations have their unique goals as well. Still there are specific goals which all Jedi have and seek to accomplish. They are again born of the fiction, but proven themselves useful and beneficial. These are very basic concepts and can be picked out of almost any Star Wars media.

    The goals are simple. The first goal is simply continual training. To be capable of fulfilling the role of the Jedi in everyday life. The second goal is to provide support. Something which can be accomplished in a variety of ways. The third goal is to render aid, a bit different than our previous goal. Which will become more clear when we explore it a bit further. The fourth goal is to defend those in need. Another broad goal with many ways to accomplish it. The last goal is to further one's understanding of the Force. This is basically a reminder of spiritual well-being. This concept will be more clear in a bit as well.

    Purpose is important to any endeavor. Without a purpose we are just wandering through life aimlessly. This applies to all we do. When we set goals for ourselves there becomes a purpose for our actions. In life there is a reason why we do what we do and follow the ideals we follow. This of course applies equally to the Jedi. Direction is needed to keep focus on living as a Jedi. We are not Jedi just to be Jedi. It has a purpose, it has direction, and that is what we find with the five goals of the Jedi. These are common goals which all Jedi strive for regardless of affiliation. Everyday Jedi seek to fulfill all five of goals and sometimes more.

Each morning is a new chance to meet and accomplish these goals. Remember these are simply the core basics.

Train Diligently:
I've worked too hard and too long to let anything stand in the way of my goals. I will not let my teammates down and I will not let myself down. ~ Mia Hamm

As is usually prudent we will start at the beginning. Goal number one, "Train Diligently" which is often accompanied by the following: "*Be capable of fulfilling the role and course of a Jedi.*" When I was training under Mindas Ar'ran in Great Falls, MT. he would say it daily, "train diligently." It was an idea that if you wanted to excel then you needed to follow this. If you wanted it to be second-nature then you must train daily. If you are to be capable of fulfilling the role and ideals of the Jedi then you certainly have to train diligently as a Jedi.

First we must be capable. We must be able to handle the tasks which we seek to undertake. We want to be able to guide and live our own lives in a positive and beneficial manner. IN order to do that we study, we train, practice, and ultimately live by the ideals of our path. Thus we state it clearly, Train Diligently. This application in everyday life is simple - because you should be doing it daily.

Jedi training covers a wide variety of practices from meditation to physical fitness. They each have a reason for being practiced and they are tied closely to the Jedi ideals. As an example, serenity is tough to accomplish without a basic practice of meditation. This ideal becomes very self-evident within the first week of Jedi training. Thus goal number one, in order to ensure the other four goals listed can be accomplished, we seek to be capable of fulfilling them.

This is why Jedi spend years training. It is not easy to alter our lifestyle to include more activities. Life gets busy enough without adding in extra work, studies, and practices on top of it. It is essential however that we do, if this is the life we chose to live.

Waking up in the morning to meditate and have a light work-out isn't really second-nature to most of us. We have to train ourselves to get into the mindset of better living. Of doing something good for ourselves before we go out and face the world everyday.

Training helps us approach problems and situations as a Jedi. No one is born a Jedi, just as no one is born a Police Officer or President. You can be suited for it, you can excel without trying, but you need to prepare for it, train for it, learn the practices, procedures, and ideals. The best way to excel is to train day-in and day-out. This is why the first goal of any Jedi is to train diligently.

Provide Support:
In a relationship each person should support the other; they should lift each other up. ~ Taylor Swift

Listed and explained as "*sometimes the best help, is merely encouragement and support. A Jedi does not always have to be hands-on, but instead provides the needed support.*" Jedi through their training often become pillars of strength. This can be emotionally, spiritually, mentally, and even physically. Because of this many people often turn to the Jedi for support. Whether that is advice on a difficult matter, how best to proceed in a certain situation, discussions on faith/belief, or even just knowing they are capable in moving furniture instead of their 85 year old Grandmother. It is all about being relied upon to support those in need.

People often confuse a Jedi's desire to help others and be of service to mean they volunteer 100% of their time. Or that they should all be members of the Peace Corp. You do not need to look far and wide to find places to help and people who could use a little support. From local community projects to friends in a bad place, there are many places a Jedi can provide their support.

How can we provide support? So many ways. By supporting a friend's decision. By being a shoulder to cry on and reminding people how strong and capable they truly are. By seeing the good and the positive in those around us and reminding them of their value. We want to enforce their foundation, remind them they are good, with or without anyone. We can support them by helping in endeavors, by picking chores when they are bogged down. A spouse is buried with work - you pick-up their chores until things mellow out. Give them some time to rest and regain themselves. This works with friends, school as well. It is simply about temporarily picking up some of the burden and supporting a person through a tough time. While letting them have self-reliance and gaining from the experience which life has given. You can support your community with liter pick-up, park clean-ups, and so forth. Truly the only limitation is your own desire and imagination.

Most of us do this in our lives regardless. Jedi just tend to actively look for the opportunities and chances to act on it. This serves as a reminder that Jedi do not have to be 100% pro-active and go off to every corner of the world to be of service. There are plenty of chances to lend our support right in our own inner-circle. There are many ways for Jedi to be of service in our lives. Whether that is simply a shoulder to cry-on, being the objective adviser on career choice, or picking up some chores around your friend's house because he injured his back. Sometimes it is as simple a few words of encouragement. Just have to look for the chance to offer that support.

Render Aid:
The race of mankind would perish did they cease to aid each other. We cannot exist without mutual help. All therefore that need aid have a right to ask it from their fellow-men; and no one who has the power of granting can refuse it without guilt. ~ Walter Scott

Explained as "*Sometimes it is resources that are needed the most. A Jedi can give their time, money, services, and/or supplies for the service of others.*" We are not always in a position to give of ourselves. Sometimes we just do not truly have the time or ability. When considering of how to be of service to the community (and the world at large) we can look at rendering aid. This is meant to remind the Jedi that while we seek to help others and better the world there are many great organizations out there already doing just that.

Render Aid is an easy application. Lets rephrase it - Community Service. This can be donating money, clothes, can goods, toys, blood, et cetera. This can be volunteering at any number of service projects. Teaching to Read, helping homeless families find a job and housing, working at an animal shelter. Truly many organizations and causes out there to get involved in. I like projects which seek to treat/eliminate problems rather than simply throwing a band-aid on them. Like putting schools and water purifying devices in Africa rather than simply giving bottled water. Which is more of a personal preference, obviously both render aid. This speaks to the point that there are many ways to render aid.

We do not always have the time or money to fulfill this area. So we seek to combine it. Support, Aid, Jedi Ideals, and Your own Fun - example I ran a Spartan Race and personally raised money for a good charity organization. This one act had a direct and beneficial impact on many areas of the Jedi Path (physical fitness, render aid, etc.). So you can certainly find a way to accomplish many things at once without burying yourself in needless activity.

The idea here is that we have a variety of ways to help out. Donating our blood and/or plasma to a local group such as Red Cross. Giving yearly monetary donations to groups like the Salvation Army. Giving our time and helping local organizations such as the Optimist or Rotary clubs, making sure their events have enough people to flourish. Donating food, can goods, and clothing to groups like Goodwill and local homeless shelters. Plenty of ways to render aid to our world.

The Jedi do not need to be a humanitarian organization themselves. They simply need to be willing to help such preexisting groups out and truly there are a plethora of ways to accomplish that. Sometimes a Jedi may live in an area where a natural disaster occurs, here they can also render aid by helping with sand bags, clean-up, search and rescue, and so forth. What we seek to impress here is that a Jedi can find many ways to render aid and help world-betterment, even on a small scale. The key is to find a group and way that speaks to you. That you feel comfortable giving your time and resources too.

Defend Those in Need:
Non-violence leads to the highest ethics, which is the goal of all evolution. Until we stop harming all other living beings, we are still savages. ~ Thomas A. Edison

This next goal has the longest explanation because it can be easily misunderstood. "*Sometimes people need help defending themselves. Whether that is by sticking up for them in a argument or unfair situation. Calling the proper authorities to correct a situation. Or showing that they have someone who will not allow physical harm to come to them. A Jedi defends those in need.*" Like our previous goals, many ways to accomplish this concept.

Defense of others has long been an accepted and understood part of the Jedi Path. Yet due to the way the fiction represents Jedi many take defense of others to be a purely physical act. People have visions of physically fighting in the place of another. Fighting injustice against law-breakers and "evil-doers". All these really way-out-there scenarios in which a Jedi must pick up a sword and fight. Which is simply not the case. This tends to lead others, even some Jedi, to the wrong conclusions about our Path and what we seek to accomplish.

Jedi seek to defend those in need. True enough, but what is defense? Who is in need? What is the best way to handle the situation? Consider these questions for a second. It should help really put the idea into perspective. Often times simply a kind word in a heated situation is all that is needed. Some humor injected into a tense situation can change the entire dynamic. Sometimes it is simply standing up for someone getting picked on. Whether that is by a friend, family member, boss, co-worker, classmate, and so on. Often times just voicing an opinion can resolve a situation.

Application of defending those in need can be foggy. Most people automatically start getting visions of lightsabers dancing in their head. It is not about combat. Can it be? It could, in the worse case scenario - violence could be what is hinted at here. But there are many ways to defend those in need. Helping at an Animal Shelter is a great way to defend those in need. Animals are in need, they require protection. That often just means food, water, and shelter, perhaps funding and work at a shelter to keep it going. Someone willing to be a voice for the voiceless.

It could be showing verbal support for a person being picked on or bullied. Letting them know that they are not alone. That they do not have to accept that as a way life. That you can and are willing to defend their character, their life. It can mean defending an innocent person from prosecution. It can be defending one's religious freedom. You can defend one's sexual freedom. The Earth is in need of defense is it not? Environmental Protection groups (decent, legit ones) can be a place to put your defending muscles to work. Endangered Species. Truly there are a lot of things in this world that could use a champion. Defend those in love, those chasing a dream, those fighting everyday simply to see the people they love smile. None of this demands physical or violent defense.

One last application of defense - calling the proper authorities. Remove the bad element, not simply push it onto someone else. Don't play hero, instead be a hero by getting the right people involved to ensure a difference is made. A good defense can be getting the right offense in there. Get the people trained to handle the situation involved.

This is why diplomacy is a core practice of Jedi. Because we understand that sometimes the best defense is prevention. It is resolution achieved through words. It can be in siding with an individual and letting them know they are not alone. If they seem incapable of standing up for themselves sometimes just having another do so for them can resolve the situation. As well as give the person the courage and example to stand-up for themselves later on. How one does that is why Jedi study Conflict Resolution, so as not to turn a bad situation into a worse one.

However hostile situations can arise and a Jedi may find themselves confronted by a very aggressive and violent individual. This is why physical fitness and self-defense are a part of the Jedi Path and practices as well. Again though, many ways to reach peaceful resolution. So many things are factored into such potential physical confrontations. Jedi are prepared for the worse, but look for the better options. For example, calling the proper authorities always a viable option. I cannot stress that enough.

It is a goal of the Jedi to defend those in need. From the planet, to animals, to our fellow humans. Make no mistake, there is a large variety of ways to reach this goal. Many which tie into the two previous goals. Which is a staple and of the Jedi Path. We have this continual theme of this tying with that, that tying in with this, and so forth. This is one of the more tricky goals simply because of the broad scope it entails and the concern over physical confrontation. Hopefully we have conveyed that there are many peaceful ways in fulfilling this goal and those options should always be practiced and sought first. Understand we are not talking about swinging lightsabers at the problem. Remember - <u>The best Jedi will never be in a physical fight.</u>

Study of the Force:
That deep emotional conviction of the presence of a superior reasoning power, which is revealed in the incomprehensible universe, forms my idea of God. ~ Albert Einstein

Our last goal is briefly described as "*A Jedi continues the study and advancement of the Force. Further defining the Force, by continually experiencing, exploring, and understanding it.*" The Force is a very difficult subject to discuss for two major reasons. The first being that it is ineffable. The second being that it is terminology taken direct from Star Wars which has little to no definitive elements. Even the movies have varied in the explanation of the Force.

For the Jedi the Force is a core concept, yet it is a fresh concept for us. It is a new element that allows us to approach age old questions in a new way. Most religions, philosophies, and beliefs, have something similar attached to them. A mystical or metaphysical element which they have explored and have formed a general consensus on. The Jedi Community as a whole does not have a singular stance on the Force. As we have already covered. Some Jedi prefer to go with the vague explanation provided by George Lucas via the character Obi-Wan Kenobi in Star Wars A New Hope, *"an energy field."* Some connect the Force with their already established religion or belief, e.g. they view the Force as the Holy Spirit. Same thing, just a different name. Such as viewing the Force as the Chinese concept of Qi (Chi), simply using a different label.

The reality is that the Force is unknown to us and as a whole we have left it open to personal interpretation. Yet we continue, as a whole, to explore the ideas, concepts, and science behind the Force. What is it? Are there abilities and knowledge to be unlocked from it? Where did it come from? How is it connected to life? Is that the same or different than the explanations provided by the fiction?

The one thing we cannot deny is that the Force is core to the Jedi. Both fictionally speaking and speaking from an inspirational standpoint. Not to mention that many Jedi feel the Force is key to advancing our studies and path as a whole. We have made leaps and bounds on the philosophical front of our Path since 1998. Now we need to seek to have a better understanding of the more spiritual and mystical element to our Path.

Application of Studying the Force is simple observation and reflection. It is a very personal subject. As such it is one I cannot give you answers on. The Force is Ineffable - it is left for you to explore, experience, and thus define. You must find your answers through open, honest, and sincere study. Let your exploration, your experience, guide you while you seek the objective, calm, and focused mind which will provide the best answers. Boldly explore new concepts and ideas and find your answers. Meditation, Prayer, following the other Goals, do not ignore the concept of the Force. Develop it.

In the future this will no doubt become critical information which will help us find similarities in our diverse field. The Jedi Path is very young, we are just beginning. As we grow and explore individually, the more we gain and obtain pieces of the overall puzzle. Eventually we will be in a much better position in the future to offer more information. To provide core ideals on this ineffable force which we hold to be invaluable to living as a Jedi. So study, explore, experience, and find your own definition, then be willing to share and discuss with other Jedi. In this we may all learn from one another and use our diversity as a strong tool in our progress.

It is a continual goal of the Jedi to advance their understanding, both individually and collectively, of the Force. Our current focus is ensuring that individual understanding. Encouraging Jedi to affirm their views, beliefs, and definitions. To solidify their views on such matters. To weigh the variety of views which exist and are currently being explored, tested, and studied. Is the Force more biological, perhaps relating to Mitochondria? If so does that take anything away from the more mystical elements and ideals or does that perhaps open a new venue of understanding?

In the end it is a core subject which our scientific knowledge and personal understanding is rather limited. Especially considering paths and beliefs out there which feel they already know the answer to such subjects. So we encourage the continual exploration, advancement, and experience of the Force. Our goal is simple – never stop exploring and advancing our understanding of the world and mysteries within it.

Conclusion

Learn from the past, set vivid, detailed goals for the future, and live in the only moment of time over which you have any control: now. ~ Denis Waitley

The Jedi Way is found in living. One cannot be a Jedi by hiding from life. As much as we would often like to simply disappear to some Temple in the middle of nowhere this is hardly living as a Jedi. The fictional Jedi were not removed from the hustle and bustle of everyday life. Their main staging grounds were at the heart of civilization. They were traveling among average citizens and they continually were sent out to help deal with major issues.

It is the feeling of the Jedi that these concepts can be of use, of benefit, and of positive enforcement in our everyday lives. It is an idea that how we live, what we live by, and what we do with our lives truly means something. It does have an effect in the world, if only a small one. But a small positive change, a bright example of humanity is so much better than none. It is not about changing how the world works. Rather it is about changing how we work with the world. *"Let everyone sweep in front of his own door, and the whole world will be clean."* - Johann Wolfgang von Goethe

These are the basic goals which we hold ourselves too. This is the simplest overview of these goals. As one can imagine we could go much deeper into each subject. Yet I simply want to offer this basic and well-known outlook. This book is not meant to be a training manual. It is only meant to offer understanding into what Jedi do and how we live. That said, let us look at some of the practices which Jedi partake in on a daily basis.

Practices

I've always considered myself to be just average talent and what I have is a ridiculous insane obsessiveness for practice and preparation. ~ Will Smith

The practices of the Jedi are daily exercises which Jedi follow. They are vague concepts to allow for a variety of ways to complete them. Meditation can be completed on a daily basis in any number of ways. This is why they cross over all Jedi groups and are done by each person living as a Jedi. Some groups do have very specific means of accomplishing these practices. Including their own meditation and physical fitness routines. Though most take a 'whatever works for the individual' approach to the subjects.

For this book we will not be offering specifics. You won't find any lessons, exercises, or assignments to follow. You can find such advice and recommendations at any Jedi group or you can purchase more of my books which cover these topics in a more instructional manner. I prefer the second option of course, your pocketbook will no doubt prefer the first. Back to being serious, this is simply an overview of the practices of the Jedi. We'll explore a bit about why we incorporate these ideals, how they help us in our daily lives, and how different Jedi accomplish them.

These subjects are multifaceted concepts which relate to the Jedi in various ways. Awareness for example is not just about being aware of your surroundings, but emotional, motivational, and situational awareness as well. As I have mentioned before, each of these topics can have their own book on them in relation to the Jedi alone. This is evident by the fact that these subjects do have a plethora of books on them, in the general sense, already. The goal here is simply to help you understand what Jedi do and why they do them. I offer this more for those who are considering following the Jedi lifestyle. I doubt these practices will sway the argument for the Jedi being a religion or not in either direction. I do feel that they offer insight into how the Jedi live their lives. Which certainly helps in determining how you personally classify the Jedi. And since you made it this far into the book I have to imagine you have some interest in the Jedi and the classification associated with them.

I want to stress the importance of finding guidance in these areas if you wish to follow the Jedi lifestyle. There are plenty of free resources available online, not to mention a local library can be of great help as well. Remember that these are generalized and the focus of the Jedi is personal well-being and improvement. There is no one-size fits all way to approach these topics and you will need to put in the proper research and work for these concepts to be of maximum benefit. Which brings us to our first practice of the Jedi Path.

Self-Discipline:
We all have dreams. But in order to make dreams come into reality, it takes an awful lot of determination, dedication, self-discipline, and effort. ~ Jesse Owens

Simply the core to any endeavor you wish to excel in. You need self-discipline in order to achieve your goals. Whether you want to be an all-star football player, the best salesperson, or a kick-butt Jedi, you are going to need self-discipline. No one can give self-discipline, there is no ten step guide. Well, I mean there are ten steps guides, but at best it inspires; it does not give you self-discipline. Only one person determines whether or not you have this attribute (that person is you, if that is not clear). The thing is, you are never too young or too old to acquire self-discipline. For some it comes more naturally, sometimes a by-product of their upbringing. For others self-discipline is a constant struggle to complete day-in and day-out.

I personally fall into that second category. My base nature

is very lazy, but that is not something which has produced the results I want. If you want to succeed you have to put in the work. You have to be willing to put other things on hold, dig in, and focus on completing what you need to get done. This book I can easily use as an example. I am tired from work, I am tired from working-out, I want to veg-out and kill some brain cells playing a video game or something. However my goal is to write about this wonderful path which I live. So, I set aside a certain amount of time each day for writing and the only person responsible for ensuring I adhere to that schedule is myself. It is a matter of self-discipline. Especially when writing is the last thing I want to do.

    This is simply my most recent example. For other Jedi it is physical fitness that taxes their self-discipline the most. They don't have the motivation to get it done, but they acknowledge it is a core part of being a Jedi. It is good for them and helps them lead a healthy lifestyle, so they power through. They hold themselves to a schedule, ensuring that they complete their daily practices. The practices and goals of the Jedi are constant tests of Jedi self-discipline. This is simply because they often require more out of our day. They are not things which are easily completed in the course of the day and require us to put in extra effort to ensure their completion.

    I can list inspirational quotes, tips on time-management, ways to be organized, to set-up a fluid routine. You know, the ten step guide approach. Certainly all of these things can help in the process of maintaining self-discipline, but they cannot make you follow-through on any thing. You can create the best schedule and have everything organized, but if you do not adhere to it then it is all a waste. In the end self-discipline is simply getting up everyday and doing what you need to do, regardless of how you feel about it.

    There is not one successful Jedi that does not follow this practice on a daily basis. This isn't to say Jedi don't partake in the occasional lazy-day. We all need our downtime, it is a core part of staying sane. What we are saying is that self-discipline is simply something Jedi do on a daily basis. In fact most people do without realizing it. Doing the dishes when you do not feel like it, helping a friend out when you'd rather not, going into work when the bed is much more inviting. We are often displaying our ability to complete tasks despite our current feelings about the task.

This isn't some abstract concept which is outside our abilities. Truly, I am the laziest person I have ever met. My desire to accomplish anything is nearly non-existent, but I do it because it is required of me. I am confident in saying that if I can do it, anyone can. Motivation, goals, passion, desire, these certainly help us in embodying this concept, but they are not necessary to do so. Regardless of desire, you can still wake up each morning and accomplish your to-do list. You may not like it, you may not enjoy it, but you can certainly do it. You just have to push forward or as the old Nike slogan went, just do it.

Awareness:
What is necessary to change a person is to change his awareness of himself. ~ Abraham Maslow

Awareness is another one of those multifaceted concepts within the Jedi ideals. There is a focus on personal awareness which covers emotional and motivational. There is a focus on outward awareness, your physical surroundings including situational and social surroundings. Awareness is practiced daily as a way to take in the world around us. As well as to reflect on how we react to the world around us. It is one thing to understand the world we live in. It is another to understand how that affects us and how we feel about it.

Emotional awareness is the biggest focus. If emotional well-being is the foundational stone of the Jedi, we must we aware of our emotions. As well as our emotional reactions to the world around us. Certain things affect us in certain ways. Knowing this allows us to counter ourselves when people seek to push our buttons. If I tell my friend that having to repeat three times will automatically annoy me and thus make me angry. He will in fact seek to make me repeat myself several times, just to get a reaction. There are plenty of people like this. Someone who will push buttons just for the enjoyment of it. It is a form of control that they can exercise over people. If you know what makes someone angry, you can use that against them.

The way such buttons lose power is by being aware of them. Knowing and understanding our reactions helps us regain the power over them. If my knee-jerk reaction to repeating myself three times is frustration then understanding why will help me overcome it. It also allows me to be aware when someone is obviously using it just to get a rise out of me. In this knowledge we can rise above and render those buttons powerless.

This principle applies outwardly as well. Taking in our surroundings we can feel comfortable in knowing where things are. Exits, fire extinguishers, A.E.D. Machines. Or just knowing where the bathrooms are can ease the mind tremendously. Keeping awareness minimizes our chances of getting lost. Noting landmarks, signs, and the direction you are heading can help you find your way around new places. One of the better places to test that is an amusement park. Noting where you been, where you going, what is around you, you can confidently navigate the park like you live there. Which can ease the stress of such visits.

Being aware of your surroundings extends to paying attention to other people. This helps in our diplomacy and communication. Being aware of the moods of others can ease our interactions with people. Being playful when someone is in a bad mood can cause friction. You don't have to adjust your mood at all, but often adjusting your approach can make all the difference in the world. But first you have to be aware. We deal with this on a daily basis, Jedi or not. Co-workers, fellow students, teachers, parents, siblings, there is always someone in our life in which we want to be mindful of their feelings.

If self-discipline is the first step, awareness is surely the second. After-all how can we help, fix, or address something if we aren't even aware of it?

Meditation:

Meditation is all about the pursuit of nothingness. It's like the ultimate rest. It's better than the best sleep you've ever had. It's a quieting of the mind. It sharpens everything, especially your appreciation of your surroundings. It keeps life fresh. ~ Hugh Jackman

Sit down, shut up, and just listen. This is what I tell myself when I am falling behind on my meditation practice. Meditation is often a misunderstood thing. Often images of uncomfortable sitting positions and monks on a cold mountain come to mind. Really it is just about giving ourselves a few precious moments to allow our minds to unwind honestly. Allowing the thoughts to flow openly, freely, and reach a state of quiet harmony.

Meditation is not that complex. It is about focus. Focusing on breathing, focusing on a spot on the wall, focusing on inner thoughts, focusing on a mental image. Plenty of techniques and methods which all help the mind to process the information of the day.

I want you to really consider how much noise and information you are bombarded with daily. Background conversations. televisions, cell phones, games, music. All the imagery which we don't consciously process. We have all this stimuli flooding our senses on a near constant basis. It is a wonder all of us aren't completely insane. Yet our minds have defenses, we don't pick up on everything. Our brains tend to filter through the information as our body rests. As the Dalai Lama once said, *sleep is the best meditation*. Contradicts the starting quote I know. The concept is simply one of allowing the mind the process information and become stable once again. Meditation does this as does a goodnight sleep.

Meditation allows us to regain ourselves. In the hustle and bustle of it all we can get swept away in the emotions of a situation. We can over react to one thing because of something else that is bothering us. When we meditate we are calming the mind to re-focus and allow those feelings and emotions to wash through us. It is not uncommon during deep meditations to feel and release emotions. This can be in the form of crying or laughing. We are stopping and those important feelings can finally be acknowledged and released. This is absolutely core to our emotional well-being. It is simply not healthy to leave all that emotion bottled up.

Consider how many paths and ideals use meditation. There is a reason for it. Not some oobie magical reason. When talking about mental health, meditation will come up. When talking about emotional health, meditation will come up. When you are talking about physical health people will bring up your mental state which in turn – that is right – brings up meditation. It is used by many because the effects can be seen and experienced nearly right away. It is necessary that we give ourselves time to process our feelings and experiences. That we just give ourselves time to breathe. Meditation gives us a tool to accomplish that.

Meditation can be done in a variety of forms and you have to find what works for you. Often just taking a couple minutes to breathe can do wonders. I have a app on my phone which is a meditation reminder. It rings a little chime for two to five minutes. I use it especially on busy days. It just allows me a couple minutes to stop, breathe, acknowledge my thoughts, and slow down just for a moment. That is often enough to center myself and continue on with the rest of my day. Yet I always make time for meditation at the end of the day. It simply has proven its worth. Emotionally, mentally, physically. Meditation simply provides its benefits freely and visibly. This isn't something you have to take anyone's word on. You try it for a week, you'll notice a difference. Others will notice a difference.

The key to remember about meditation is that it isn't about enlightenment. At least not for us non-monastery living folks. It is simply a great and wonderful tool in ensuring our personal well-being on several levels. It is a daily practice that repays you. You don't have to put in two hours a day sitting on the floor staring at a blank wall. Seek 15 minutes alone time everyday – you'll understand why we practice this. It simply provides the Jedi with the best possible foundation to grow from. It is simply an invaluable tool that cannot be ignore.

Now I know I have said a couple times this is not a training book. However since I shared my little physical pick-me-up in the morning. I figure I will share a favorite meditation of mine. It is by Osho, who is by far my favorite source on meditation. Unless we are talking for more educational purposes than Eric Harrison gets the nod. Anyhow, I feel this highlights what I was saying about meditation and may help you understand better why we as Jedi incorporate meditation as a daily practice. Noting of course that understanding comes from doing, not reading.

Osho Meditation from the *Art of Tea* – The mind disappears whenever you stop planning for the future. The mind is nothing but a projection of the future. It disappears when you start living moment to moment. Live moment to moment. For three weeks, try.

Whatsoever you are doing, do it as totally as possible. Love it and enjoy it. Maybe it looks silly. If you are drinking tea it is silly to enjoy it too much – it is just ordinary tea. But ordinary tea can become extraordinarily beautiful – a tremendous experience if you can enjoy it. Enjoy it with deep reverence. Make it a ceremony. Making tea... Listening to the kettle and the sound. Then pouring the tea... smelling the fragrance of it. Then tasting the tea and feeling happy.

Dead people cannot drink tea, only very alive people. This moment you are alive! This moment you are drinking tea. Feel thankful! And don't think of the future. Next moment will take care of itself. Think not of the morrow. For three weeks live in the moment and see what happens.

Good stuff right? Osho has a lot of books. You can find him anywhere. He is very free-spirited. For a more western understanding and explanation – Eric Harrison. Jedi or not meditation is a great practice to incorporate.

Diplomacy:
Take advantage of every opportunity to practice your communication skills so that when important occasions arise, you will have the gift, the style, the sharpness, the clarity, and the emotions to affect other people. ~ Jim Rohn

Diplomacy is a bit of nomenclature which can be misleading. Certainly diplomacy is the idea and goal. But what we are really talking about is Communication. Effective communication can bring a peaceful resolution to just about any situation. It is about being able to communicate clearly, effectively, and most importantly in terms the individual can understand. When you are mediating or seeking to resolve conflict of any kind (e.g. a dispute between friends), you have to communicate in a way that people will understand and respond too.

The best peace-keepers are ones who know how to communicate to the individuals they are dealing with. Diplomacy certainly has other elements involved. Knowing when to compromise and when to hold your ground. It is important in any diplomatic (or conflict resolution) process to be as fully armed with information as possible. The more knowledge you possess the better. It is about having the tools and resources to back-up any claims, trades, etc. that you might use in negotiations. But tops on all of that is being able to communicate. What good is having knowledge and resources if you cannot effectively communicate that to those you are dealing with?

Sick of the word communication yet? From easing a potential bar fight to discussing bills with the spouse, it all comes down to communication. You have to be able to express yourself in a manner that allows your message to get across clearly and effectively. That doesn't necessarily always require words. You can communicate your love for someone in a plethora of ways. Just as you can demonstrate your displeasure in a variety of ways. However – the key to that communication is understanding. Just because your actions are clear to you, does not mean they are clear to the other person.

When I was married my wife and I were going through a hard time. During which I woke-up every morning (during that time) and made her tea. For me it was my way of communicating that I cared for her and her needs came before mine. I never said that however and that communication was lost in the problems we were dealing with. Communication is not a one-sided act. It needs follow-up, confirmation, and you do need to get verbal (or written) 99% of the time.

If you can grasp this principle of open, honest, and clear communication you'll find diplomacy second-nature. When you can effectively communicate with those around you conflict becomes easier to resolve. Of course this is one of those things where it sounds easy, but is harder to translate into your daily life. It can be difficult to clearly express our thoughts and feelings. It can be even more difficult to express them in a way that others will understand. Yet it is always worth trying. Especially in a relationship. Sometimes you may have to find a different way to say/communicate what you want and/or feel. Worth it though.

Conflict is often a product of misunderstanding. Usually when we can clearly understand where someone is coming from we can resolve the issue. Now resolution is a matter of acknowledgment and coming to a mutual agreement. You do not have to approve, agree with, or even like something. But that doesn't mean you cannot acknowledge and accept something. This goes the other way as well. You do not always need someone's approval or agreement, but simply the acknowledgment and acceptance.

Diplomacy is one of the more underutilized aspects of the fictional Jedi. Personally I'd love to see a Jedi novel where it is pure political intrigue. Regardless this was a facet of the fictional Jedi, dealing with politics and mediating important government disputes. They were often called in as third-party diplomats. We seek to fulfill the concept through our daily lives with general conflict resolution. The best way to do that is with preventive measures. Being clear in our – say it with me – communication is obviously the main method we encourage. You can also take mediation courses and conflict resolution materials abound on the internet.

This is simply the ideal that states we can resolve just about any situation with our minds. That we do not have to resort to any sort of violence. That we are capable enough and clever enough to talk our way through the most troubling situations and still find a win-win for all involved. And what is the main component for that? Communication.

Physical Fitness:
Physical fitness is not only one of the most important keys to a healthy body, it is the basis of dynamic and creative intellectual activity. ~ John F. Kennedy

My second favorite practice of the Jedi – physical fitness. For me it is tied with meditation on helping with mental and emotional health. I love to get a good work-out when things are getting a bit stressful. I enjoy using my heavy bag to help ensure I am not bottling up any emotional stress. Of course there are times when it feels like a chore. When I just don't want to be active. This is usually cured by doing something active, but fun. Something as simple as a game of ping-pong or air hockey.

Many people hear (or read) physical fitness and automatically think of going to the gym seven days a week for three hours each day. There are plenty of ways to stay physically active without all of that. From a daily pick-up game of basketball to walking your dog in the hills. The idea is simply to find something active which you enjoy doing. Something that doesn't require a whole lot of effort. I mean you can enjoy kayaking, but if you have to travel and go through a lot trouble to accomplish that then you won't want to count on it for your daily physical fitness.

As we have brought up several times before physical well-being is simply key to overall personal development. This isn't about looking like a model or lifting 500 lbs. It is simply about keeping fit and staying healthy. That level of fitness varies for everyone and there are a plethora of ways to accomplish a daily fitness goal. You simply have to find what works for you.

Something I like to incorporate is an easy exercise routine each morning. I am talking 10 push-ups, 15 sit-ups, 20 squats, and then off I go to brush the teeth. Something quick, easy, no stress. It is nothing. Doesn't even account as exercise, but it helps me start the day off right. And should the day get busy and I find by the end I am just not going to work-out? I feel a tiny bit better knowing I at least got in my morning routine. That tiny peace of mind does wonders for my stress levels.

Blood flow, oxygen in-take, keeping the joints moving, any physician can lecture us until the end of time about the benefits of physical fitness. We all know it, most of us just don't care enough. It has been a long and crazy day. Last thing one wants to do is exert themselves more. Still it is something infinitely useful and beneficial to us. As Jedi we force the issue on ourselves. That is why we push finding something fun. Wii Fit, Kinect Boxing, these are perfectly acceptable as well. Be creative, have fun, and it won't be a chore. You might actually enjoy it. Maybe even start to look forward to it.

This isn't to say Jedi don't take days off or have the occasional lazy day. Simply that we know the value of physical fitness to our overall well-being. There is a interconnectedness to it all. One affects the other. Each plays an important role in our lives. It is great to take those days off. They are needed for the sanity at times. Likewise staying active also does wonders for ones sanity. As Bruce Lee said, *"Jogging is not only a form of exercise to me, I is also a form of relaxation. It is my hour every morning when I can be alone with my thoughts."* So get out there and partake.

My Journey

Go confidently in the direction of your dreams. Live the life you have imagined. ~ Henry David Thoreau

I mentioned that becoming the best version of you is a staple of the Jedi Path. I am still young and have a lot of life ahead of me. I know that I'll continue to find a better version of me as my journey is not over yet. But this also means I have seen some pretty awful versions of myself as well. No one is born a Jedi, no one is born perfect, we all have to struggle and learn as we grow. I don't remember a whole lot about my childhood. I imagine that is mostly by choice. The things I do remember are not always the best. As much as I am willing to get into my journey there are things I cannot talk about because they involve people close to me who are still alive. It is too easy to misunderstand, point fingers, and pass blame. So understand that I am being vague on purpose, but I feel it is important to know that my journey as a Jedi was not and is not an easy one.

I, like many other people in the world, have been searching for various answers in life. Nothing really clicked for me during my younger years. I was raised a Methodist since I was born. When I was a teenager I became a Catholic going through confirmation with my friend. In my late teens and early twenties I studied Buddhism, Taoism, and Jainism. I was searching for answers to the bigger questions. I was also looking for purpose. I was looking to feel like I belonged in this world, that I had a place and role within it. Despite my search nothing ever stuck with me. Eventually my aspirations won out and I settled on the idea that I could become a Jedi. That didn't happen overnight however and it wasn't something I embraced immediately.

When I was a young child something happened to me. Someone I cared about was under duress and they called out my name. They called for my help. Being a kid I had always imagined myself the hero. I'd spend hours outside defeating the bad guys and saving the day. It is, of course, a different thing for a child to experience the reality of being called upon. I did not help, my fear lead to my decision to stay exactly where I was. The event ended as well as it could have and no serious harm was done, but it stuck with me. Not in a good motivational way, at least not at first, but more in feeling like a failure.

Now to be clear, I fully understand the situation now. I have a good understanding of the Fight, Flight, or Freeze reflex in adrenaline driven situations. I have long since discovered inherently my reflex is freeze (my reaction time isn't the best). I get that being a kid, there wasn't anything I could do to help in that situation anyhow. It was simply one of those things that sticks with you, but never really needed to. Now this event is simply me acknowledging where my drive to be better comes from. Of course, that is one incident, whereas my whole childhood pushed me toward the Jedi Community as well (emphasis on community).

As a kid I never had a lot of friends. I usually had one friend and was on good terms with all their friends. Human nature being what it is I often found myself alone. I never really fit in to any group or label or classification. I wasn't smart enough to be a nerd. I wasn't dark enough to be a goth. I wasn't tough enough to be a jock. I wasn't funny enough to be the class clown. I was a person who floated through life having no idea where I was going nor did I even care.

I was introduced to Star Wars around 10 years old. The Empire Strikes Back. I thought it was boring, except for one part. Dagobah. Every scene with Yoda had me captured. I couldn't really tell you why per se. Maybe the format, maybe how it was presented, I watched those scenes and to my young mind I thought I could do the same. The Jedi in Star Wars simply seemed to embody everything I wanted to be. Calm, wise, capable, even though there seemed to be a sadness about them. Jedi – that was my answer. So that is what I pursued and focused on. That was fun. I was running in the backyard, climbing and swing from the tree, and trying to lift rocks with my mind. It doesn't provide direction to a lost life however. Just a new way to play hero. While those ideals presented in Star Wars helped me focus on something greater, my life hadn't changed. I had upped my book collection, had an interest, but I was still with one friend or no friends at any given time. I was still not part of a group. I was a loner. Like most who struggles with their place in life I thought about a more permanent solution (yep, suicide). My attempts were childish and didn't go far, but that only made me feel like more of a failure. This continued through High School when I finally had enough and simply quit going to school. I stopped going and no longer cared about any sort of future.

    At this time I found a group. Still no label which would fit. We weren't a gang or a crew, we were simply kids who were having fun, but ultimately we were short-sighted. We never had our eyes to the future. We lived day by day, enjoying the moment, thinking the future would sort itself out. One of our artistic outlets was graffiti art. We had rules, never private property, had to be a show of talent, not just spray painting letters. We sought to get into magazines with our work. A few other rules which we felt put us a step above your average kid with a spray can. Since these things were often against the law, it was truly only a matter of time until we were arrested. Eventually my turn came, but something happened first. In 1997 the Star Wars trilogy was re-released in the theaters. Watching the Empire Strikes Back on the big screen re-ignited that search and desire for something more. So I began to go to Barnes and Nobles everyday to read books on subjects I felt were Jedi-like. This included Eastern Philosophy like the Tao te Ching, Zen Buddhism, as well as various sources like Bruce Lee's Striking Thoughts. I started to add Meditation and Physical fitness into my daily life. These things began to empower me.

    Empower the bullied without guidance and they will become the bully. I was stronger, I was in more control, I was no longer afraid. That meant I no longer had to take anyone's garbage. I became a voice that people listened too. I began to determine how events unfolded and ended. I was no longer a lost loner with no friends. I was a person who people worried about. What will I do? How will I react? But as said, empowerment without guidance is dangerous. When we are hurt and are given the power to harm those that caused us pain, most of us will take it. Especially in the teenage years when our bodies (hormones) are getting the better of us. I lashed out, I was violent for violence's sake. I exercised my new found power simply because I could. I never had that before.

Well, that is not true. Of course I had that before. We all have that ability and power in us from the very beginning. I simply never knew that. I did recognize that simple fact. Many who are bullied don't understand that have the power and capabilities to stand-up for themselves. We are not powerless. Yet I did not know that then. So as a hurt kid I misused my newly embraced empowerment. Which lead to some very poor decisions.

As I said, my time would come to be arrested and it did. I was caught and sentenced to community service and probation. In 1998 my probation was up, however I had broken the rules of my probation. Which lead to the inevitable conclusion which was I was sentenced to juvenile camp. The Judge seeing I could use a sense of responsibility sent me to Fire Camp. It is a camp where you fight Wildland fires and when not doing that, cleaning up county property (clearing brush, removing fire hazards, trimming tress, etc.). I spent close to a year in Fire Camp and it did have a effect. The effect was directly related to the decision I had made before I went to camp. I wanted to be a Jedi. I wanted to make my childhood dream a reality. I knew I wanted to do something worthwhile with my life. I knew I wanted to give back to the community. I knew I wanted to use that self-empowerment in a good way. I just didn't know how. The Jedi Path had given me the desire to do something good. I could have easily fell into that repeat offender trap. The mentality is surprisingly tempting. Yet I was inspired to reach for something more.

This also gave me time to do a couple of really needed

things. First I earned my High School diploma. Second I reflected on the nature of the Jedi ideals I had been involving myself on. I decided I wanted to be a better person, to be a Jedi, not the person who allowed their pain to control their actions. I began to really examine the principles I had twisted to justify my previous actions.

When I got out of fire camp I went searching for the Jedi. I found role-playing sites for the most part. A couple sites though presented the material in such a way that I began to believe that becoming a Jedi was a viable option. By 1999 the Jedi Community had bloomed due to the release of Episode One. Ironically one of the more disliked movies, but that is neither here nor there. I became an extremely active member of the Jedi Community at this time. I dedicated my entire being to becoming a Jedi. When I went to college I majored in Philosophy, because is that not a core part of being a Jedi? I took Eastern Religion classes to supplement my Jedi training. At the time Buddhism and Taoism were a huge part of the Jedi Community curriculum. My dedication paid off, by the end of 1999 I was granted the title of Light Jedi Master and Inner Council member. While I was proud, it didn't feel right. I didn't feel ready for the responsibility of leading and teaching others. So I left briefly, fortunately a loss of internet also aided this decision. As when internet returned, by curiosity got the better of me and I checked back I to see how things were progressing.

When I returned a couple months later I decided to understand as much as I could about the Jedi. So I began to join several different Jedi sites. The Jedi Community had grown with the excitement of Episode One. By the year 2000 I was a member of several sites, the number varying between 10 to 20 active websites. I sought and was accepted as a student at all of them. I wanted to understand, to learn, and to grow. It was a wondrous time to be a part of the Jedi Community, if not a bit chaotic. Like all things there were good moments and bad moments. There were things I can look back at and smile. Then there were things which broke my heart and made me wonder about humanity. It was simply a time of open and honest exploration as children. Make no mistake, regardless of age, we were children.

Overall it was a good time of sharing experiences and knowledge. This helped me in my journey of becoming a Jedi. There were so many like-minded individuals. We shared ideas, experiences, and techniques. We had our Jedi Temple, it was simply online. After years of searching and feeling left out I finally had a label, a group, a community in which I belonged. A bonus was that it was one that didn't carry the possibility of living my life in the penal system. There was a child-like sense of wonder with it all. It was nice to have a home.

Of course that was the problem, like empowerment. Having a sense of community after years of not having any takes some adjustment. I lost myself to the online world of the Jedi Community. Friendships, rivalries, romance, despite being words on a screen the feelings and emotions were real. The majority of my time and life was spent in this online world. As you can see, I was still the child with unrealistic expectations. By 2001 the Jedi were my life. It was simply where I spent all my time. That carries its own drawbacks.

Something happened in 2001 however that even the Jedi Community was not expecting. The 2001 census including the United Kingdom, Australia, New Zealand, and Canada had close to half a million people list Jedi as their religion. This caused a bit of a stir in the media. One of the sites I had come to call home was the Jedi Creed. A place that was very open and truly enjoyed the fictional side of Jedi. Sure they had serious philosophical discussions on self-betterment and helping in your community, but they also enjoyed role-playing and discussing the movies. Well in light of the census phenomenon a BBC reporter came to the Jedi Creed to see what this Jedi stuff was all about. However he did not talk with any of the members. Simply looked over the site, read some subject headers, and made his judgment. The Jedi Creed did not truly survive the fall-out. They say there is no such thing as bad press, but for kids looking for answers to bigger questions with one another, there truly is bad press. So the Jedi

Creed closed its door and some people left the Jedi Community. But one website does not make up the Jedi Community and the leadership of the Jedi Creed had already been working on other projects such as the Jedi United. So the Jedi Community continued on, but with a new element added Religion.

Prior to 2001 no one in the Jedi Community really called their path a religion. In fact many felt the Jedi Path supplemented their religious beliefs. This new development created a rift in the Jedi Community. A religious focus versus a philosophical focus; Jediism versus Jedi Realism. As I mentioned before I had spent a lot of time looking at religion for my answers. I didn't feel religion was the way to go. I had found answers or at least breadcrumbs of answers, while simply being a Jedi. Realism, Jediism, just more division, more unnecessary labels for people to claim answers they did not truly have. It was here in 2001 that I felt and believed that *the journey for answers was in fact the answer.* Such fortune-cookie wisdom certainly seemed appropriate for the time. The division has lasted over a decade, as if such labels truly matter. Some groups have taken steps to be recognized as an official religion. Such as the Temple of the Jedi Order being incorporated as a non-profit religious corporation. Yet I never got behind the whole idea that being a religion made the Jedi way valid.

Of course when you care deeply for something and don't even know why, you are in a dangerous situation. As I have said, we were all kids, regardless of age. This means there came a time when we were no longer able to play nice together. The events above simply added strain on our already overburden minds. I felt betrayed. I became hurt and disillusioned with the Jedi Community. So like any child I acted out. I wanted to be a Jedi, to learn with Jedi, to hangout with Jedi. Instead I was seeing myself and others for what we were, children playing Jedi online because we were trying to fill a hole within ourselves. It seemed the rest of the world saw us that way too. That realization was not something I was ready or prepared to face. I lashed out, I acted against the Jedi ideals, in other words I took my ball and went home.

There was just one small problem with that. The small fact that from 17 to 21 I had done basically nothing with my life. All my focus had been on being a fictionalized version of Jedi. The Jedi Community was all I had which meant I had nowhere to go. No career to focus on. No offline relationships to focus on. So it was not long (a couple of months) until I came right back to the Jedi Community to continue on. Couldn't give-up by then, had invested too much. Or at least that was my line of thinking at the time.

In 2002 I was offered a chance to live with some other Jedi in Montana. This was the turning point for me. They helped me get my life moving forward. A full realization that being a Jedi wasn't just ideals and concepts, but how you applied them to your everyday life. Jedi wasn't a career, it didn't pay the bills, Jedi was how you lived. It was how you went to work, how you approached school, what you did with your free time. It was here that the pieces of the puzzle all began to fall into place. The Jedi still had a lot of room to grow and so did I. Yet the seeds had been planted and we were beginning to finally grow.

We failed more than we succeeded. We tried various teaching methods. We sought simply to copy the work of other greater minds and more established paths. People simply taught the Tao te Ching. Or they copied lessons form New Age books. They used the works of Carl Jung or Joseph Campbell to make up for their lack of material and knowledge. As a community we couldn't address simple questions or solve simple problems. We continually divide ourselves because our differences were more important than our similarities. This meant that personal growth stagnated. How can you grow in a healthy manner if your environment is not healthy? Our community was one of politics, drama, and backbiting. We all wanted something more, something better, but because none of us had lived it long enough we couldn't agree on how to proceed forward together.

This is where I began my journey of "for Jedi by Jedi." An ideal that in order for us to evolve and grow as actual Jedi we must work on Jedi-specific material ourselves geared directly toward other Jedi. The Jedi Circle was created under this concept. This of course took a more trial and error approach. Does this Jedi concept truly benefit me in my everyday life? One way to find out. Ouch, no, not useful. Rinse and repeat through all the material that inspired us to carry the Jedi name to begin with. This was a process of years. By 2007 I thought myself set and knowledgeable in the Jedi Way. I had been actively seeking the Jedi ideals for 10 years. I was good or so I thought. Then I met a girl who made me realize how much I had avoided myself.

See, it is really easy to focus your attention outwardly. A lot of problems in the world. A lot of things that require fixing. Despite the Jedi Path being what it is, a path of self-betterment, there is a focus on serving others. The pitfall is that you continually and always look outwardly. Fixing other people's problems and never addressing your own issues. I was a great Jedi on the surface. I did community service. I gave of myself when needed. I continued to work on Jedi Community issues. What I did not do was ensure that I was in a place to do all of that. I had focused on the Jedi Community, not on me as a Jedi. My efforts were geared outwardly. They were projects on fixing the community rather than fixing myself. Something that will catch up with anyone eventually. You have to solidify yourself first – then take on the world.

In any case I was lucky enough and unbelievably happy to eventually marry that girl I mentioned. She believed the outward work matched the inward work. That I was in fact a Jedi through and through. When the reality came crushing down we were both crushed. We both were not in a position to handle it. We both had spent our time looking outwardly and found that we were incomplete. It was rough, as divorce usually is. It was a wake-up call that there was a hole in the Jedi Path. Service alone was not what made a Jedi. It is not the the Jedi Ideals failed me. It was that I had failed me. The community had failed to be what a community is suppose to be, especially ours. We as a community allowed the outward pursuit of the Jedi stop us from fully developing ourselves from the inside out.

World-betterment through self-betterment. That is the motto. We follow that simple concept now. We work from the inside outward. We must be in a position to help others before we rush off to do so or we are just building a castle on sand. I had learned it the hard way. It is easy to get lost the feeling of helping others. It is tough to look within and face the things we would rather forget about. Being a Jedi is about being the best version of you possible. You cannot do that if you are simply focusing on everything, but you.

Like everyone I have had varied experience throughout my life. I have lost good friends. I have only ever truly been in love three times in my life and each one ended painfully. These were results of me not knowing who I was. Not acknowledging my own feelings and my own desires. I lost myself in belonging to a group. The funny thing is that as I grew so did the Jedi Community. Not because we are or were tied together, but simply because time and experiences was needed for growth. We had to go through the fire. These bad experiences were necessary for both of us to see that change was necessary. I needed to change how I approached living as a Jedi and the Jedi Community realized some of the methods were flawed in helping Jedi become their dream.

We have both have come a long way since 1997. We have had our dark moments. We have had embarrassing moments we'd rather forget, but know we can't. We have come to understand that in order to truly be of service to the world around us, we must first ensure that we are capable of doing so. Our well-being is core to how we interact with the world and society. Physical, Mental, Emotional, Spiritual, Social, Environmental, Financial, all of these are core areas of well-being that each Jedi now faces in their training and development. It isn't about just shoving someone out the door and saying, *"do or do not; there is no try."* There is an understanding that in order to embody the concept of Jedi, we must continually work on our well-being. Bettering ourselves everyday and living by the concepts in our daily lives.

For myself it has been ten years of the same ideal.

Searching for answers through the Jedi Path. Whether one wants to call that a religion, a lifestyle, or philosophy makes no difference to me. I had my fights, my debates, my arguments with people in the Jedi Community over such semantics. In the end the category isn't important. Are the Jedi a religion? Does it matter? What changes with the answer? Is a yes any different than a no? For the past 15 plus years I have dedicated my life to being a Jedi. The answers I have found, the things I have learned, the experiences I have had, they do not change based on whether or not someone labels Jedi a religion.

Ultimately that is why I am still here. Merit, validity, things I can point to and say, without the Jedi I wouldn't have made it. The ideas of the Jedi saved my life more than once, in a literal sense. Truth be told I have failed more than I feel I have succeeded. There are plenty of times in my life where I failed to act like a Jedi. I failed to adhere to the ideals of the Jedi Path and suffered because of it. The mixture is there though. Where I can, throughout my life, pinpoint beneficial reasons why the Jedi Path is worth living and worth following. I imagine this is the same for any one regardless of the label they wear. Where we look back and can see the positive and negative influences in our lives. For me the Jedi has been a positive influence that has lead to many worthwhile accomplishments in my life. Such as graduating the Police Academy.

That is my vague journey and it hasn't been easy. It could be easily used to point out the flaws on the Jedi and myself. The fact is we were both children playing with diamonds. We did not understand the value of the tools we held in our hands. We are older now, wiser through the pain of experience. What I went through is not typical nor is it something that would happen today. If the Jedi were then what they are now, my life would be extremely different. That is the beauty I see in our future. The simple fact that the Jedi Path can and has helped people achieve exactly what they wanted out of life. They are happy and working towards their dreams with full support and knowledge. Of course I am not even close to being done in my journey. I started the Jedi

Academy Online web-group in 2007 to explore the merits of living the Jedi lifestyle. In doing so I have the learned tough lessons in responsibility, leadership, and accountability. My understanding of the Jedi Path has grown even more due to running the website. The journey continues and it is one that has proven useful to me.

The simple fact is this. I'd be dead or in prison if not for the Jedi. Nothing else spoke to me and nothing else inspired me. I was able to meet the love of my life through the Jedi. We may no longer be together, but we did have some good moments and I do not regret those. I have met some great people and made some great friendships. I have grown into a man who is emotionally, physically, socially, spiritually fit. I am good in those areas because of the Jedi ideals. I was a complete wreck before. I have faced my demons and laughed with them. I now have full confidence in overcoming the challenges in my life. And I am overjoyed at the fact that my journey, the good and the bad, has and continues to help people become the best version of themselves as well. I simply offer this brief overview and reflection as a small insight into how one Jedi came to carrying the name. Why I chose to continue to carry the name. It is my hope that this shows that there is worth in anything that provides someone with positive and beneficial growth. Jedi is a name, the path itself is one of world-betterment through self-betterment. After 15 years I am really still in the self-betterment department. Physical, mental, emotional, spiritual, social, environmental, and financial well-being is a constant development though and truly lasts a lifetime. It is my hope that when my time is done I will have accomplished something of that world-betterment goal. Even if that is simply bettering the Jedi Path for the next generation grow from.

Closing Thoughts

I still find each day too short for all the thoughts I want to think, all the walks I want to take, all the books I want to read, and all the friends I want to see. ~ John Burroughs

When I first decided to write this book I had something completely different in mind. It was meant to be much more about explaining and validating the Jedi. I wanted to use my journey as a stepping stone into why this is a useful and beneficial path. I wanted to show that just because someone says they follow the Jedi Religion are is no reason to write them off as delusional. That there are tangible experiences which prove the viability and benefit of living as a Jedi. People want to point and laugh at Jedi as if it is truly different than any other religion or belief out there. Sure there is something a bit silly about holding onto a name from a science-fiction franchise, but that does not automatically invalidate the concepts behind it.

The thing is when I began to write my focus shifted. Originally the *My Journey* section was at the forefront of the book. It was meant to be much more detailed, with names, places and events being specifically addressed. I was planning on highlighting the struggles I faced in my life and how the Jedi ideals helped me be a better person in detail. Showing that without the Jedi my life could have been very different and very dark. Instead I realized I was not interested in sharing my story, at least not in-depth at this time. I realized that not only is validation a pointless waste of time, but I am far from a finished product. Fact is, if someone wants to laugh they are going to laugh. The Jedi Path speaks for itself. I find that by simply sharing the very basics of our path with those interested they will come to their own conclusion. I ultimately left in the my journey section because I figured why not get a better understanding of the person writing this book. Yet it simply highlights while we, as Jedi, have come far we still have a long road ahead of us.

I have not found all my answers in life, but I am only 32. I have a lot of life ahead of me barring unforeseen circumstances. There is one thing I know with great certainty. The Jedi lifestyle is my answer to living in this crazy world. It is what keeps me focused on the greater good and reminds me of the benefits of helping others. It keeps me working on self-improvement and it is a potent reminder when I am spending too much time at the computer. Were I alone in this, one might be able to write it off as a personal issue. However there are hundreds, if not thousands of people who have found answers, meaning, and purpose within the Jedi Path.

Isn't that what counts? That regardless of the name there is a path out there that is speaking to people to reach for more. To be more, to help others, and live a beneficial life. For some reason the older religions and concepts did not stick, they did not grab the attention of these people. They, like myself, were lost in a sea of uncertainty. For some reason Jedi spoke to them and helped them find something worthwhile. Encouraged them to live healthy and positive lives. Not only for themselves, but for those around them as well.

One can debate the merits of the Jedi being an actual religion. I have certainly done so on numerous occasions. One can debate whether a non-profit religious tax exempt status with the United States Internal Revenue Service makes a group an actual religion or not. But all of that is simply superfluous to the fact that the Jedi has proven beneficial to those who have lived by it. Sharing personal stories is one way to go in demonstrating that. Still I find that if you put the core concepts to paper and let the reader decide using common sense and rational thinking they will come to the same conclusion. Maybe it is not for you, but certainly if it works for some else then the name is a small matter.

It is not about believing or disbelieving in a God. As mentioned before many find the Jedi supplemental. That it works well with their beliefs, be that Christian or otherwise. It is about believing in something greater than ourselves. Something which is left to each individual Jedi to identify for themselves. It is that beautiful diversity which has given us some great insights and allowed us to grow as individuals.

Self-Discipline, Integrity, Responsibility, Accountability, Service to Others, surely these ideals speak for themselves. One can say that the Jedi are fictional, but the ideals and practices they represent are certainly real. Are they exclusive to the Jedi Path? No, but the Jedi Path does incorporate various ideals in a unique way. There is a very broad view within the Jedi that is sometimes lacking in other paths. One finds they are supplementing continually to fill holes. This fitness, this diet, this meditation practice, this spiritual belief, mixing and matching from all over. Many Jedi, like myself, have found that by living the Jedi Way we do not need to engage in such practices. We have built an encompassing foundation from which to grow from. Something we have presented in this book in its most basic form.

Being a Jedi may sound a questionable, but when one understands what it means to live the Jedi Way all of that disappears. Like all things it is the actions of the Jedi that will define us as group. We are young. We have only truly started to build our path. We are adolescents who have great potential to grow into the shoes of our inspiration.

It may have been more interesting to read the little dramas over the years. Or to read about my own specific successes and failures throughout life in relation to the Jedi. It might have provided a better case for the value of living as a Jedi. It might have even made a better selling book, chronicling the ups and downs of trying to become a Jedi. That is simply not my style however and it is my hope that this more systematic approach has provided the information necessary to make an informed opinion.

Resources

My formula for living is quite simple. I get up in the morning and I go to bed at night. In between, I occupy myself as best I can. ~ Cary Grant

Training and Interactive Websites:
     First thing first – in my book anyhow. If you are interested in discussion, exploration, delving deeper, and/or training in the Jedi Path I invite you to explore one of our websites. I'll offer only two websites for your consideration. Only two as to help provide a proper introduction to the path. Some sites are a bit more risque than others. These two sites provide your baseline comparison.

    1.) **The Jedi Academy Online** – This site gets top billing for one specific reason. I created it and control the academic approach and material. As such I can fully vouch for the content and offer guidance in relation to its material. It is not an easy place. We have a different approach than most Jedi sites. We do not use titles like Knight and Master. Our standards are tough and our training program requires a good deal of time and effort. We are not Jediism nor Jedi Realism. We do not prescribe to *isms* at all. All are welcome regardless of religious views and beliefs, especially concerning the Jedi. Website: http://jediacademyonline.com

    2.) **Temple of the Jedi Order** – It would be remiss of me not to include one of the more known and active Jedi Religion websites. I cannot speak on their training or administration, but I can say if the Jedi Religion is your focus this is the place. You will find training, you will find activity, you will find Jedi. There are Jedi Religion specific web-groups, but this is your gateway. From here you can venture out if you so chose. Since 2005 the Temple of the Order has been inseparable from the Jedi Religion movement.

Website: http://www.templeofthejediorder.org

Source Material:

There are certain Star Wars materials I highly recommend. Not only for entertainment value, but also to examine for philosophical validity. Can Jedi ideals presented within them be applied to everyday life? This is where we as a group started. We had nothing but the fiction and had to develop outwardly. It took time, effort, and lots of trial and error. This is where we get the basis of our training programs. By looking at and examining the fiction are validity and then testing that within our lives. As we close in on two decades of this dedicated study we are able to offer grounded and well-rounded training concepts to living as Jedi. Yet one should not simply forget the roots. Our inspiration is still important and something I still find to be enjoyable entertainment. So here are my recommendations which helped me develop the material in this book.

The Jedi Code:

If you are looking for a fictional take on the Jedi Code you can explore the concept further in the books – Power of the Jedi by Wizards of the Coast (ISBN 0-7869-2781-X). Jedi Academy Training Manual by Wizards of the Coast (ISBN 9780786951833). The Jedi Path by Daniel Wallace (ISBN 9781603800969). The first two books by Wizards of the Coast will also cover the Jedi Rules of Behavior and list them together as one and the same.

For non-fictional look at the Jedi Code. You can check out the Jedi Academy Online books. Specifically the Tier One Program (ISBN 978-1470003555 or ISBN 978-1482339710). Or you can simply go to the Jedi Academy Online website (jedicacademyonline.com).

The Jedi Circle:
There are no fictional sources on the Jedi Circle. It was created for actual Jedi by actual Jedi. An example of being inspired by fiction, but shaped by reality. There is the old Tier Two program from the Jedi Academy online in book form, simply called The Jedi Circle: Jedi Philosophy for Everyday Life (ISBN 978-1475083248). In time I hope to have more available, but for now, this is it.

Likewise you can once again simply go to the Jedi Academy Online website (jedicacademyonline.com). This provides you a platform in which to interact with Jedi. Ask questions, explore various concepts, and get a deeper understanding of the material.

Jedi Inspiration:
There are a lot of good books out there on Jedi ideology and thought. Not all are stories, but I found them fun to read regardless. In any case these are some of my favorite Star Wars Jedi related books. Power of the Jedi (ISBN 0-7869-2781-X), Jedi Academy Training Manual (ISBN 9780786951833), Jedi Apprentice entire series (by Jude Watson), The Jedi Path: A Manual for Students of the Force (ISBN 9781603800969), Star Wars Jedi vs. Sith (ISBN 9780345493347), Star Wars Cloak of Deception (ISBN 9780345442970), Star Wars Revan (ISBN 9780857689009), and any of the movie novelizations.

General Reading:
Here are just a books I personally recommend for general reading. Some these may be up your alley, others not so much. They span many years for me, so the subjects touch on various topics I had an interest in at one point or another. *The Hiding Place* by Corrie ten Boom, *Meditations* by Marcus Aurelius, *Withcraft Theory and Practice* by Ly de Angeles, *Meditations* by Osho, *Gates of Fire* by Steven Pressfield, *The Warrior Ethos* by

Steven Pressfield , Any Meditaiton book by <u>Eric Harrison</u>, *Tao of Jeet Kune Do* by Bruce Lee, *Art of Shen Ku* by Zeek, *Show Me How: 500 Things You Should Know* by Lauren Smith, *Pragmatism: A New Name for some Old Ways of Thinking* by William James.

Offline Resources:

Offline resources depend greatly on your location. Jedi are world-wide and usually very willing to meet up with more like minded individuals. If you reside in California, USA you can join the California Jedi Meet-up group (which I am a member of). Website: <u>http://www.meetup.com/CaliforniaJedi/</u> There are several groups of Jedi which meet-up in-person. Such as in Chicago, IL, USA. So whatever Jedi website you decide to join (if you do) you can ask if there are any groups or anyone is in your area. Even with Jedi, treat it like all online interactions. Be smart, be safe, be sure your first meet-ups are in public places. Make sure people know where you are and who you are meeting. Outside of that Jedi offline resources are rather limited at this point in time.

Disclaimer:

My poor excuse for covering my behind in regards to legal matters.

Part 1.) Copyrights and Trademarks: All original material printed here is protected on the individual and Organizational copyright laws of the United States of America (2013). Any reproduction or unauthorized use of the material contained herein is prohibited without the express written permission of the Authors and Publishers.

Jedi Academy Online materials, including all books and websites are not owned, operated, or in association with George Lucas, Lucasfilm Ltd., or Disney Inc. The materials in this book are only used and only will be used for Educational Purposes. All else is strictly prohibited. STAR WARS, THX and all logos, characters, artwork, stories, information, names, and other elements associated thereto are the sole and exclusive property of Lucasfilm Ltd. and Disney Inc. All copyright and trademark items are used without consent for educational purposes only under the Fair Use Act.

The creation of any other materials derived by the authors of this book and the Jedi Academy Online is expressly used for private, non-commercial viewing purposes. The individual writings exist for the benefit of the visitor and are copyright of the Author and the Jedi Academy Online. If any violation is detected, please contact us immediately.

Part 2.) Professional Advice: The Jedi Academy Online (referred to as JAO herein) and Kevin Trout are not engaged in rendering medical advice, and the contents of this book are not intended to take the place of such advice. Please consult a physician and/or physical therapist before using any of the information, advice or any of the services within this book.

My Thanks:

To all who have picked this book. Likewise special thanks to all of you who are reading this. Special thanks to George Lucas, of course. Jaden, Pace, Jasta, Morken, Talon, Sirius, Silver, Zenon, Chrissy, Andy, Mindas, Arkai, and Joshua. To all Jedi at the Jedi Academy Online. To Carolyn and Dennis for allowing me the chance to chase my dreams.

www.ingramcontent.com/pod-product-compliance
Lightning Source LLC
Chambersburg PA
CBHW071312060426
42444CB00034B/1976